The Beginner's
BIBLE QUESTION & ANSWER BO
is great for...

- ★ Your own personal Bible learning and enjoyment—and fun for your parents too!
- ★ A Bible knowledge game with your friends (see page 5)
- ★ A "Family Fun" night—or a refreshing change-of-pace for Family Devotions
- ★ A guide for Bible studies on important Bible themes and characters
- ★ A fun travel-time brightener during long trips in the car
- ★ A Bible learning tool in Sunday school and children's church, vacation Bible school, Christian schools, home schools, children's church, Bible clubs, etc.

ATTENTION: PARENTS—Younger children will benefit greatly from your help in guiding them through this book (and *you'll* benefit as well!)

THE BEGINNER'S BIBLE QUESTION AND ANSWER BOOK

Cover Design by Steve Diggs & Friends, Nashville

PRINTED IN THE UNITED STATES OF AMERICA

International Standard Book Number: 0-945564-21-X

Most Scripture quotations are from
the *New International Version*
and the *International Children's Bible*

Also quoted is *The Living Bible*

For information, write to:
Questar Publishers, Inc.
Post Office Box 1720
Sisters, Oregon 97759

QUESTAR PUBLISHERS, INC.
SISTERS, OREGON

THE BEGINNER'S

Bible Question & Answer Book

MACK THOMAS
Illustrated by BEN ALEX

A Few Words about This Book...

★ "TO HELP YOU LEARN AND ENJOY THE SCRIPTURES MORE"—that's the reason this book was written. So you'll probably want your Bible open beside you as you continue in this book.

★ Yes, some of the questions are hard. But if you already knew every answer, there would be nothing here to encourage you to open your Bible and enjoy the good things you'll find there on your own!

★ The questions get harder as you go from the first section in the book (the blue, one-star section) to the last (the purple, five-star section). So here, as in most things, the beginning is a great place to start!

★ **You'll find answers for all the questions in the back of the book**, but first try looking them up in the Bible. You'll discover many more interesting things there than you will on the answer pages.

★ Most of the Bible verses in this book are quoted from the *New International Version*. There are also lots of verses quoted from the *International Children's Bible* (also known as the *New Century Version).* Just a few verses are quoted from *The Living Bible.*

Using The Beginner's Bible Question & Answer Book as a Group Game—

for 2 or more players

- Have this book open, and your Bibles handy.
- For four or more players, divide into two teams; players within each team work together to answer questions.
- On each turn, one side (the Questioner) selects *one* of the questions from this book, and asks it to the opposing side (the Answerer). After the Answerer gives a reply, both sides look together at the correct answer in the Bible or in the back of this book. Then the other team or player becomes the Questioner.
- The choice of questions is up to the Questioner, but the Answerer can choose the difficulty level—one-star, two-star, and so on.
- The Questioner must give any accompanying Bible reference along with the question.
- You may want to set a time limit (adjusting it as necessary) for answering each numbered question. The Answerer can try to find the correct answer in the Bible during the time allowed.
- SCORING: One point for each one-star question answered correctly, two points for each two-star question, three for each three-star question, and so on.
- EXTRA SCORING:
  — One extra point for each question answered correctly without the Answerer having to look it up in the Bible.
  — One extra point for each question answered correctly in the "Gold Star Special" sections.
  — Two extra points for each question answered correctly in the "Extra Exercise" sections.

Introducing:

You'll see Zeb and Zeba popping up often on the pages of this book, always wearing and doing something a little different...

JUST FOR FUN, answer the questions on the next page as you allow Zeb and Zeba to help you get better acquainted with this book. *(Answers are printed upside down at the bottom of the next page.)*

- Find the page where Zeba is wearing a red "sash" belt, and pulling a broom. On that page, there's a four-letter word starting with "C" that's repeated SEVEN times. What is that word?
- Find the page where Zeba is wearing an orange head covering, a green belt, and a robe with yellow sleeves. On that page, there are five questions that all begin with the same word. What word is it?
- Find the page where Zeb is wearing a blue-and-yellow sash belt, a yellow head-band, and a green robe with a red hem around the bottom. His bucket is full of water. There are four questions on that page that all begin with the same word. What word is it?
- Find the page where Zeb is wearing a green robe and a golden head-dress, and he's reading something. There's a question on that page that has the names of two colors in it, and the correct answer is the name of a third color. What are those three colors?

1—page 229, and the word is "Creation"; 2—page 191, and the word is "I"; 3—page 155, and the word is "Who"; 3—page 61, and the colors are black, white, and gray

1

Faces and Places

The Sovereign Lord will wipe away the tears from all faces.
(Isaiah 25:8)

1. A man just woke up, and his face looks happy. In a dream, an angel told him to marry a woman named Mary. The angel said Mary would have a baby, and the baby would be God's Son. Who is the man who had the dream? **(To find his name in the Bible, look in Matthew 1:20–21.)**

2. This baby has a crying face. A princess found the baby in a basket floating on the River Nile. Who is the baby? **(Exodus 2:1–10)**

3. A man and a woman are hiding in a garden. Their faces are sad. They ate something that God told them not to eat. They've never been afraid before, but now they are. What are their names? **(Genesis 3:1–20)**

WHERE ARE WE?

4. We're in a place where big, hungry, dangerous animals are kept. Suddenly, through an opening above, a man is dropped in among the animals. But they don't bite him, because an angel comes and shuts the animals' mouths. *Where are we?* (DANIEL 6)
5. We're in a place where a young boy, who appears to be about twelve years old, is talking to some older men who look like teachers. They are surprised at what the young boy is saying. Then a man and a woman with searching faces come into the room. When they come closer and see the boy, they rush to him and say, "Jesus, we've been looking everywhere for you!" *Where are we?* (LUKE 2:41-52)
6. We're inside a place that is always very dark and very damp, and it smells fishy. A man is here, praying to God. He sounds as though he's sorry for something he's done. He can't get out of this place on his own, but after three days, he'll suddenly come out fast! *Where are we?* (JONAH 1—2)

▼ ▼ ▼

7. The faces of this man and woman are very old, but they are also happy and laughing. They are holding a baby boy. He isn't their grandson, and he isn't their great-grandson. This is their very own child, and they name this baby Isaac. Who are these happy parents? (GENESIS 21:1–7)

♥ Does *your* face look happy today?

Don't know an ANSWER? Look first in the Bible, then in the back of this book...

I have called you friends, for everything that I learned from my Father I have made known to you. (***Jesus****, in* J*OHN 15:15*)

JESUS, THE HOUSE GUEST—

1. When Jesus visited Peter's house, a woman there was sick in bed with a fever. But Jesus touched her, and the fever left. Who was this woman? (**MATTHEW 8:14-15**)

2. Jesus and His disciples had dinner at the home of Matthew the tax collector. The Pharisees didn't like this, because of who else was there. Who else was there? (**MATTHEW 9:10–13**)

3. There was a noisy crowd at this house, but Jesus sent them out. When He told them why He was sending them out (it had to do with a little girl who was inside), they laughed at Him. What did He say to them, and why did it make them laugh at Him? (**MATTHEW 9:18–26**)

4. While Jesus was in this rich tax collector's house, the man told Him he would pay back four times the amount of money that he had cheated anyone out of. Who was this man? (LUKE 10:1-10)

5. Jesus was preaching the Word of God in a house in Capernaum. The house was packed with people. It was so crowded that a man who was paralyzed couldn't get in to see Jesus. His friends helped him solve his problem, however. What did they do? (MARK 2:1-12)

6. In Mark 3:20, we read about Jesus and His disciples going into a house, but they could not eat there. Why couldn't they?

7. One Sabbath day, Jesus went to eat at the house of a very well-known Pharisee. A sick man was also there, and the Pharisees were watching Jesus closely. They didn't believe anyone should do any kind of work on a Sabbath. So Jesus asked them, "Is it lawful to heal on the Sabbath or not?" Then Jesus healed the man and sent him away. Again he asked the Pharisees, "If one of you has a son or an ox that falls into a well on the Sabbath day, will you not immediately pull him out?" How did the Pharisees answer these questions from Jesus? (LUKE 14:1-5)

♥ How is Jesus your Friend at *your* house?

Don't know an ANSWER? Look first in the Bible, then in the back of this book...

They were brave warriors, ready for battle… Their faces were the faces of lions…they were as swift as gazelles in the mountains. (1 Chronicles 12:8)

ONE-WORD CLUES—Use these groups of one-word clues to help you discover the names of Bible heroes — one name for each group of clues.

Example: PRAYER • LIONS • ANGEL • SAFE

Answer: Daniel

1. ARK • ANIMALS • FLOOD • RAINBOW (Genesis 6—9)

2. PROMISE • BELIEVE • LAND • OLD • SON (Genesis 12—21)

3. ALONE • DREAM • STAIRS • HEAVEN • WORK • YEARS (Genesis 28—33)

4. COAT • DREAMS • SOLD • SLAVE • EGYPT • JAIL • LEADER • FOOD • BROTHERS (GENESIS 37-46)

5. BASKET • RIVER • PRINCESS • BUSH • PLAGUES • PHARAOH • MOUNTAIN • COMMANDMENTS • DESERT (EXODUS—DEUTERONOMY)

6. SPY • TAKE • LAND • COURAGE • JORDAN • JERICHO • WALLS • CANAAN (NUMBERS 13—14; JOSHUA 1—12)

7. SPIES • ROOF • JERICHO • CORD • WINDOW (JOSHUA 2, 6)

8. WOOL • DEW • 300 • JARS • TORCHES • TRUMPETS (JUDGES 6—7)

9. HAIR • STRONG • CUT • WEAK • GROW • PILLARS • CRUSH (JUDGES 13—16)

10. HUSBAND • DIED • FOLLOW • GRAIN • KINDNESS • REDEEM (RUTH 1—4)

11. BARREN • SAD • PRAYER • DEVOTE • ANSWER • SON (1 SAMUEL 1—2)

12. NIGHT • CALL • SPEAK • HEAR • ANOINT • KINGS (1 SAMUEL 3—16)

13. SHEPHERD • SLING • GIANT (1 SAMUEL 17)

14. PRINCE • FRIEND • COVENANT • ROBE • TUNIC • SWORD (1 SAMUEL 18-20)

Don't know an ANSWER? Look first in the Bible, then in the back of this book…

WORK TIME: Who did each of these jobs?

1. Giving names to all the animals. (Genesis 2:19-20)
2. Building an ark for keeping safe in the Flood. (Genesis 6—9)
3. Helping the people of Egypt save their food during seven good years, so they would have enough during the seven bad years that followed. (Genesis 41)
4. Leading God's people out of Egypt. (Exodus 3—15)
5. Taking God's Ten Commandments to God's people. (Exodus 19—20)
6. Leading God's people into the Promised Land. (Joshua 1—12)
7. Telling David that God wanted him to be Israel's king. (1 Samuel 16)
8. Defeating Goliath, the Philistine giant. (1 Samuel 17)
9. Building the first Temple as God's house in Jerusalem. (1 Kings 6—8)
10. Telling King Ahab that for the next few years there would be no rain in Israel. (1 Kings 17)
11. Explaining to King Belshazzar the meaning of some words written by a hand on his palace wall. (Daniel 5)
12. Going to the great city of Nineveh to tell the people to repent and turn to God. (Jonah 3)
13. Swallowing someone who at first wouldn't go to Nineveh to do what he was supposed to do. (Jonah 1)

♥ What work has God given *you* to do?

The Lord is faithful to all his promises. (Psalm 145:13)

PROMISE POWER—Match the right ending *(from the list at the bottom of the page)* to each of these powerful promises in God's Word:

1. The free gift of God...
2. And this is what he has promised us...
3. If I go and prepare a place for you...
4. Come, follow me...

(A)• *and I will make you fishers of men* (Matthew 4:19).

(B)• *I will come back and take you to be with me, that you also may be where I am* (Jesus, in John 14:3).

(C)• *is eternal life in Christ Jesus our Lord* (Romans 6:23).

(D)• — *even eternal life* (1 John 2:25).

Don't know an ANSWER? Look first in the Bible, then in the back of this book...

I will remember the deeds of the Lord; yes, I will remember your miracles of long ago. (PSALM 77:11)

1. Before the world was made, everything was dark and empty. Then God said *four words,* and suddenly there was bright light shining all around. What were those four words? (GENESIS 1:3)

2. In only six days, God made everything—the sky, the land and the seas, the sun and moon and stars, and animals and people. What did He do on the next day—the seventh day? (GENESIS 2:2–3)

3. When God made a wife for Adam, what did He make her from? (GENESIS 2:21–22)

4. I see something moist and pasty, and Jesus is putting it on a blind man's eyes. *What is it?* (John 9:6)

5. I see a staff in the hand of Moses, and when he throws it to the ground, it becomes something alive and slithering. *What is it?* (Exodus 4:1–5)

6. I see something burning, but it never burns up, and Moses can hear the voice of God coming from it. *What is it?* (Exodus 3:1–4)

7. I see Moses putting something inside his cloak; when he pulls it out, it has white sores all over it. Then he puts it inside his cloak again, and when he pulls it out, the white sores are all gone. *What is it?* (Exodus 4:6–7)

8. I see a huge sea creature—a whale or a giant fish—vomiting up a person on the seashore. *Who is the person?* (Jonah 2:10)

9. I see something large that has grown up in one day to give shade to Jonah, where he sits under the hot sun in Nineveh. *What is it?* (Jonah 4:6)

10. Someone is walking across the water toward a boat! And someone from the boat has gotten out to walk across the water to meet him! *Who are they?* (Matthew 14:25-29)

11. I see a fig tree that is completely wilted, even though yesterday it looked fine. *What made it wilt?* (Matthew 21:18–22)

Don't know an ANSWER? Look first in the Bible, then in the back of this book...

We will not fear even if the oceans roar and foam, or if the mountains shake at the raging sea.... God says, "Be quiet and know that I am God." (PSALM 46:3-10)

SCRIPTURE SCRAMBLE—WHAT GOD IS LIKE: Rearrange the words in each sentence below so that the verses read correctly.

1. *light; God is*
   darkness all. there him is no at in
   1 JOHN 1:5

2. *Lord my The shepherd, is*
   not I in want. shall be
   PSALM 23:1

3. *Lord, is the Great*
   of most and worthy praise.
   PSALM 48:1

LETTER SCRAMBLE—David, the shepherd and king and warrior, said many things about our Lord and God in Psalm 18. Unscramble the words on the right to complete correctly the opening verses of this Psalm.

4.	I love you, O Lord, my _______	*t e g h t n r s*
5.	The Lord is my _______ ,	*c r k o*
6.	my _______	*f t r r s s o e*
7.	and my _______;	*r r e i d l e v e*
8.	my God is my _______ ,	*k r c o*
9.	in whom I take _______.	*f e g u r e*
10.	He is my _______	*h e l d i s*
11.	and the horn of my _______,	*a n o t l a v i s*
12.	my _______.	*s o l t g o r n d h*
13.	I call to the Lord, who is _______	*t r o w y h*
14.	of praise, and I am _______ from my enemies.	*d e v s a*

♥ In what ways is God all of these things for *you*, too?

Don't know an ANSWER? Look first in the Bible, then in the back of this book...

Born Again

I tell you the truth, no one can see the kingdom of God unless he is born again. (**Jesus**, in JOHN 3:3)

UNLOCK THE TREASURE BOX:

What's the KEY WORD *(it goes where you see the ⁎⁎⁎)* in this passage?

____

⁎ ⁎ ⁎

(It begins with the letter "L")

"God has given us eternal ⁎⁎⁎, and this ⁎⁎⁎ is in his Son. He who has the Son has ⁎⁎⁎; he who does not have the Son of God does not have ⁎⁎⁎. I write these things to you who believe in the name of the Son of God so that you may know that you have eternal ⁎⁎⁎."

— **1 JOHN 5:11-13**

FAMOUS QUESTIONS IN THE BOOK OF ACTS

1. "Sirs, what must I do to be saved?" (Acts 16:30). Where were Paul and Silas when they were asked that question?
2. "Brothers, what shall we do?" (Acts 2:37). The crowd that gathered on the day of Pentecost asked this question of Peter and the other apostles. How did Peter answer? (2:38)
3. The high priest asked Stephen, "Are these charges true?" (Acts 7:1). When he asked this, what did Stephen's face look like? (6:15)
4. Before Jesus ascended into heaven, the disciples asked Him, "Lord, are you at this time going to restore the kingdom to Israel?" (Acts 1:6). Did Jesus answer "Yes"? (1:7)
5. King Agrippa said to Paul, "Do you think that in such a short time you can persuade me to be a Christian?" (Acts 26:28). What had Paul just said to him? (26:27).
6. From heaven, Jesus asked a man on earth this question: "Why do you persecute me?" (Acts 9:4). Who did He ask that question to?
7. Philip asked, "Do you understand what you are reading?" The man replied, "How can I, unless someone explains it to me?" (Acts 8:30-31). What was the man reading?

Be Strong in the Lord

The name of the Lord is a strong tower; the righteous run to it and are safe. (PROVERBS 18:10)

UNLOCK THE TREASURE BOX:

What's the KEY WORD *(it goes where you see the* ***) in this passage?

______
* * *

(It begins with the letter "S")

"Be *** and courageous, because you will lead these people to inherit the land I swore to their forefathers to give them. Be *** and very courageous.... Have I not commanded you? Be *** and courageous. Do not be terrified; do not be discouraged, for the Lord your God will be with you wherever you go." —JOSHUA 1:6-9

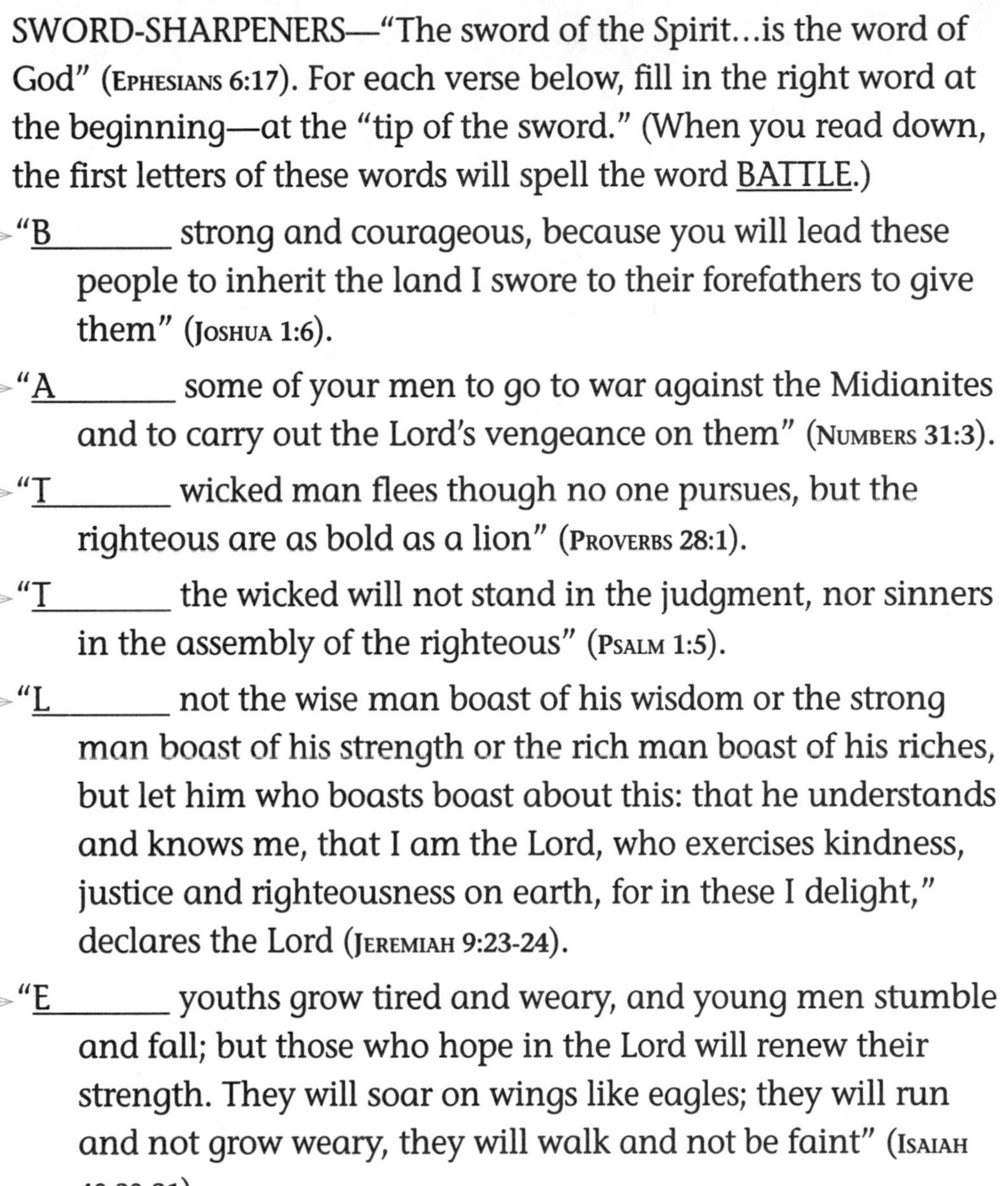

SWORD-SHARPENERS—"The sword of the Spirit…is the word of God" (EPHESIANS 6:17). For each verse below, fill in the right word at the beginning—at the "tip of the sword." (When you read down, the first letters of these words will spell the word BATTLE.)

"B________ strong and courageous, because you will lead these people to inherit the land I swore to their forefathers to give them" (JOSHUA 1:6).

"A________ some of your men to go to war against the Midianites and to carry out the Lord's vengeance on them" (NUMBERS 31:3).

"T________ wicked man flees though no one pursues, but the righteous are as bold as a lion" (PROVERBS 28:1).

"T________ the wicked will not stand in the judgment, nor sinners in the assembly of the righteous" (PSALM 1:5).

"L________ not the wise man boast of his wisdom or the strong man boast of his strength or the rich man boast of his riches, but let him who boasts boast about this: that he understands and knows me, that I am the Lord, who exercises kindness, justice and righteousness on earth, for in these I delight," declares the Lord (JEREMIAH 9:23-24).

"E________ youths grow tired and weary, and young men stumble and fall; but those who hope in the Lord will renew their strength. They will soar on wings like eagles; they will run and not grow weary, they will walk and not be faint" (ISAIAH 40:30-31).

Don't know an ANSWER? Look first in the Bible, then in the back of this book…

Bible Numbers

*How precious to me are your thoughts, O God!
How vast is the sum of them! Were I to count them,
they would outnumber the grains of sand. (Psalm 139:17-18)*

1. Jesus told a story about a man who lost one of his sheep. How many sheep did he have that were *not* lost? (**Luke 15:1–7**)

2. Jesus told a story about a man who had a son who ran away. How many sons did he have who did *not* run away? (**Luke 15:11–32**)

3. Jesus told a story about a woman who lost one of her coins. How many coins did she have that were *not* lost? (**Luke 15:8–10**)

4. How many gifts did the Magi (Wise Men) bring to the child Jesus? (Matthew 2:11)
5. For how many days and nights was Jonah inside the belly of the whale or great fish? (Jonah 1:17)
6. For how many days and nights was Jesus inside His tomb? (Matthew 12:40, 16:21; Luke 24:6-7)
7. How many of His disciples got to see Jesus transfigured in glory on the mountaintop? (Matthew 17:1-2)
8. How many of His disciples walked on water when Jesus did? (Matthew 14:22-36)
9. How many fish did the disciples catch when they went fishing together after Jesus had risen from the dead? (John 21:11)
10. How many tablets did it take to hold all the Law which Moses received from God on Mount Sinai? (Exodus 31:18)
11 How many complete copies of these tablets did God write out for Moses? (Exodus 34)

▼ ▼ ▼

How many books in the New Testament were written by…

12. John?

13. Peter?

14. Paul?

15. Luke?

Don't know an ANSWER? Look first in the Bible, then in the back of this book…

In Matthew 14:13-21 we read about Jesus giving a huge, hungry crowd all the fish and bread they wanted to eat, though He had only a little food to begin with.

16. How many fish did He start with?

17. How many loaves of bread did He start with?

18. How many baskets of leftovers were there?

19. How many people did He feed?

Some were laughed at and beaten. Others were tied and put into prison. They were killed with stones and they were cut in half. (HEBREWS 11:36-37)

POWER PASSAGE: GOD IS OUR STRENGTH—Add the right words in the right places to these verses from Psalm 46. Choose them from the list of words below (not all of them will be used).

"God is our refuge and (1) s______, an ever-present help in (2) t______ . Therefore we will not (3) f______, though the earth give way and the mountains fall into the heart of the (4) s______.... The Lord (5) A______ is with us; the God of Jacob is our fortress.... "Be still, and (6) k______ that I am (7) G______; I will be exalted among the nations, I will be exalted in the earth."

trouble Galilee story fear with know Almighty

great Adam answer sea God strength thorn fight seek

Don't know an ANSWER? Look first in the Bible, then in the back of this book...

Children are a gift from the Lord. (Psalm 127:3)

RHYME TIME: JESUS TALKS ABOUT CHILDREN—Complete these lines from Matthew 18:1-4 with the right word.

1. The disciples came to Jesus and asked, "Who is the greatest in the kingdom of ________?" *(Clue: rhymes with "seven")*
2. He called a little child and had him ______ among them. *(rhymes with "land")*
3. And he said, "I tell you the truth, unless you ________ and become like little children, you will never enter the kingdom of heaven." *(rhymes with "range")*
4. "Therefore, whoever _________ himself like this child is the greatest in the kingdom of heaven." *(rhymes with "grumbles")*

★ GOLD STAR SPECIAL ★

Which Happened First?

1. God created birds, or God created the sky? (GENESIS 1)
2. God gave Moses the Ten Commandments, or Jesus died on the cross? (EXODUS 20, JOHN 19)
3. David lived in Bethlehem, or Jesus was born in Bethlehem? (1 SAMUEL 16, LUKE 2)
4. Jonah tried to run away from God, or Adam and Eve tried to hide from God? (GENESIS 3, JONAH 1)
5. The shepherds visited the baby Jesus, or the Magi (Wise Men) visited Him? (LUKE 2:8–20, MATTHEW 2:1–16)
6. John the Baptist baptized Jesus, or Jesus went into the desert and was tempted by Satan? (MATTHEW 3:13—4:11)
7. John the Baptist baptized Jesus, or John the Baptist preached in the desert? (MATTHEW 3)
8. Jesus rose up into heaven, or the Christians were given the Holy Spirit on the day of Pentecost? (ACTS 1—2)
9. Samuel chose David to be king of Israel, or Samuel chose Saul to be king of Israel? (1 SAMUEL 9, 16)
10. Adam named all the animals, or God created Eve to be Adam's wife? (GENESIS 2)

Women in the Bible

Many women do noble things.... A woman who respects the Lord should be praised. (PROVERBS 31:29-30)

1. These two sisters had a brother named Lazarus who died, but Jesus raised him from the dead. What were the names of these two women? (JOHN 11:1-2)
2. Who was called "the mother of all the living"? (GENESIS 3:20)
3. When her cousin Mary came to see her, this woman said, "Blessed are you among women, and blessed is the child you will bear!" Who was this woman? (LUKE 1:39-45)
4. Jesus had to drive seven demons from her. Later, she was the first person to see Jesus after He rose from the dead. Who was she? (MARK 16:9)

LETTER SCRAMBLE: Hidden in the following list of strange words are some actual names of women in the Bible — written *backwards.* Find them all, using the clues below.

ASEDOL	DOJEPA	GALCOL	HAKEBER
HAMANICO	HARAS	HAROBED	IMOAN
JENELANOS	LEHCAR	LIAGIBA	MAHSEMAN
MAIRIM	OLIDAB	TELEDOB	SACROD

4. When her husband and her two sons died, she came back to Israel with Ruth, her loyal daughter-in-law. (Ruth 1)
5. She was a strong leader who served God. She went with Israel's army when they battled the Canaanites. (Judges 4)
6. She was always doing good and helping the poor. When she died, the apostle Peter raised her back to life. (Acts 9:36-39)
7. She married David after her first husband died. She worked to help both men stay out of trouble. (1 Samuel 25)
8. She was the sister of Moses and Aaron. After God led Israel through the sea to escape from Egypt, she led the Hebrew women in a joyful song and dance. (Exodus 15:20–21)
9. Jacob was in love with her, and he worked seven years for her father so he could marry her. (Genesis 29)
10. In kindness she offered water to Abraham's servant and his camels; later she became the wife of his son, Isaac. (Genesis 24:15)
11. She laughed when God told her she was going to have a son, for she was already an old woman. (Genesis 18:10–15)

Don't know an ANSWER? Look first in the Bible, then in the back of this book...

Men in the Bible

You should recognize the value of men like these.
(1 CORINTHIANS 16:18)

SMALL, TALL, TALLER

1. He was short, so he climbed a tree to get a good look at Jesus. Who was he? (LUKE 19:1–10)
2. He was Israel's first king, and he was a head taller than any other man in Israel. Who was he? (1 SAMUEL 9—10)
3. He was over nine feet tall, but still he was killed by the shepherd boy David. Who was he? (1 SAMUEL 17)

MEN OF ALL KINDS—Can you name each man?

4. *A doctor*—He went on missionary trips with the apostle Paul, and also wrote one of the gospels and the book of Acts in the New Testament. (Colossians 4:14)

5. *A farmer*— He looked for signs from God by watching a wool fleece. Then with his chosen band of 300 men he defeated the Midianites, who kept invading Israel. (Judges 6—7)

6. *A shepherd boy*— He defeated a giant, and later became Israel's king. (1 Samuel 16)

7. *A tax collector*— He followed Jesus, and wrote one of the gospels in the New Testament. (Matthew 9:9)

8. *A fisherman*— With his brother and others he left his boat and nets to follow Jesus. He became a leader of the church, and wrote two letters in the New Testament. (Matthew 4:18-20)

9. *A tentmaker*— This apostle wrote more of the New Testament books than anyone else. (Acts 18:3)

10. *A murderer*— He grew up in a king's palace, but then had to leave the country after he killed a man. God called him back, and used him to lead His people out of Egypt. (Exodus 2—3)

Our Home in Heaven

Our homeland is in heaven, and we are waiting for our Savior, the Lord Jesus Christ, to come from heaven. (PHILIPPIANS 3:20)

PLANT THE SEEDS—"The seed is the word of God," Jesus said (LUKE 8:11). In each planter-pot, plant the right "seed-word"—the word that makes the verse complete, ready to grow in your heart.

SEED-WORDS:

life star throne bride God temple dressed name

1. ______________
I saw the Holy City, the new Jerusalem, coming down out of heaven from God, prepared as a ______ beautifully dressed for her husband. (REVELATION 21:2)

2. ______________
There will be no more night. They will not need the light of a lamp or the light of the sun, for the Lord ________ will give them light. (REVELATION 22:5).

3. ______________
To him who overcomes, I will give the right to eat from the tree of _______, which is in the paradise of God.
(REVELATION 2:7)

4. ______________
To him who overcomes, I will give some of the hidden manna. I will also give him a white stone with a new _____ written on it, known only to him. (REVELATION 2:17)

5. ______________
To him who overcomes and does my will to the end...I will also give him the morning _______.
(REVELATION 2:26-28)

6. ______________
They will walk with me, dressed in white, for they are worthy. He who overcomes will, like them, be ________ in white.
(REVELATION 3:4-5)

7. ______________
Him who overcomes I will make a pillar in the _________ of my God. Never again will he leave it. I will write on him the name of my God...(REVELATION 3:12)

8. ______________
To him who overcomes, I will give the right to sit with me on my _______, just as I overcame and sat down with my Father on his throne.
(REVELATION 3:21)

Don't know an ANSWER? Look first in the Bible, then in the back of this book...

These words are like nails that have been driven in firmly. They are wise teachings that come from God the Shepherd. (ECCLESIASTES 12:11)

RHYME TIME: Name a book of the Bible which...

1. rhymes with *swan*
2. rhymes with *shark*
3. rhymes with *tester*
4. rhymes with *robe*
5. rhymes with *slumbers*
6. rhymes with *famous*
7. rhymes with *leader*
8. rhymes with *facts*

9. rhymes with *food*

10. rhymes with *duke*

11. rhymes with *spaniel*

12. rhymes with *fight us*

13. rhymes with *omens*

14. rhymes with *fudges*

15. rhymes with *flames*

16. rhymes with *truth*

17. rhymes with *pica*

18. rhymes with *playroom*

19. rhymes with *sag eye*

20. rhymes with *things*

21. with an ending that rhymes with *nation*

22. with an ending that rhymes with *nations*

23. with an ending that rhymes with *luck*

24. with an ending that rhymes with *curbs*

25. with an ending that rhymes with *shoes*

26. with an ending that rhymes with *seaman*

27. with an ending that almost rhymes with *hominy*

THE ROAD TO HAPPINESS

POWER PASSAGE—On a mountainside one day, Jesus taught His disciples about happiness (MATTHEW 5:1-12). One word we read again and again in this passage is "blessed," which means *happy*. Complete this passage below by adding the right words in the right places. Choose them from the list of words at the bottom of the page (not all of them will be used).

BLESSED are the (1) p______ in spirit, for theirs is the (2) k______ of heaven.

BLESSED are those who mourn, for they will be (3) c______ .
BLESSED are the meek, for they will inherit the (4) e______ .

BLESSED are those who hunger and (5) t______ for righteousness, for they will be filled.

BLESSED are the merciful, for they will be shown (6) m______

BLESSED are the pure in (7) h______ , for they will see God.

BLESSED are the peacemakers, for they will be called sons of (8) G______ .

BLESSED are those who are persecuted because of righteousness, for (9) t______ is the kingdom of heaven.

power kingdom crowded earth mercy
comforted early touch thirst poor God
heart kneel mountain hand grow theirs

This is what God said about the angels: "God makes his angels become like winds. He makes his servants become like flames of fire." (HEBREWS 1:7)

ANGELS AT WORK—

1. Angels with a flaming sword guarded this place so that Adam and Eve could not go in. What place was it? (**GENESIS 3:24**)

2. When an angel was there, this man's donkey could see it, but the man at first could not. Who was this man? (**NUMBERS 22**)

3. This angel told Mary that she was going to be the mother of God's Son. What was the angel's name? (**LUKE 1:26-38**)

4. An angel told these men, "Do not be afraid. I bring you good news of great joy that will be for all the people." Who were these men? (**LUKE 2:8-12**)

Bible Commands

Loving God means obeying his commands.
And God's commands are not too hard for us. (1 JOHN 5:3)

SCRIPTURE SCRAMBLE: Rearrange the words in each line below so that the verses read correctly.

1. *friends are You my*
   command. you if do what I

   JOHN 15:14

2. *your Love enemies*
   those persecute pray and for who you.

   MATTHEW 5:44

3. *Do judge, not*
   or judged. too will be you

   MATTHEW 7:1

4. *me, you If love*
command. you will what I obey

John 14:15

5. *worry Do not about tomorrow,*
about itself. worry for tomorrow will
trouble Each day has of its enough own.

Matthew 6:34

6. *Father As the has loved me,*
loved you. so have I
in Now remain my love.

John 15:9

7. *light Let your shine before men,*
your good deeds see that they may
heaven. and praise your Father in

Matthew 5:16

8. *strikes cheek, If someone you on the right*
other turn to him the also.

Matthew 5:39

9. *forces If you to go mile, someone one*
miles. go with two him

Matthew 5:41

Don't know an ANSWER? Look first in the Bible, then in the back of this book...

God Became a Man

He was equal with God. But he did not think that being equal with God was something to be held on to.... He was born to be a man and became like a servant. (PHILIPPIANS 2:6-7)

WORD GRAB — Look at the Christmas carol in the box on the next page, and "borrow" the right words there to complete all the verses on these two pages.

1. Here is a trustworthy saying that deserves full acceptance: Christ Jesus came into the world to save s________ (1 TIMOTHY 1:15).

2. He saved us, not because of righteous things we had done, but because of his m________ (TITUS 3:5).

3. And the gospel of the kingdom will be preached in the whole world as a testimony to all n________ (MATTHEW 24:14).

4. Does not the Scripture say that the Christ will come from David's family and from B__________, the town where David lived? (John 7:42).

5. The life appeared; we have seen it and testify to it, and we p__________ to you the eternal life which was with the Father and has appeared to us (1 John 1:2).

6. If anyone is ashamed of me and my words, the Son of Man will be ashamed of him when he comes in his glory and in the glory of the Father and of the holy a_________ (Luke 9:26).

7. He began to teach them that the Son of Man must suffer many things and be rejected by the elders, chief priests and teachers of the law, and that he must be killed and after three days r______ again (Mark 8:31).

8. Magi from the east came to Jerusalem and asked, "Where is the one who has been b______ king of the Jews? We saw his star in the east and have come to worship him" (Matthew 2:1–2).

Hark! the herald angels sing: "Glory to the newborn King;
Peace on earth, and mercy mild, God and sinners reconciled!"
Joyful, all ye nations, rise, join the triumph of the skies;
With the angelic host proclaim, "Christ is born in Bethlehem!"
Hark! the herald angels sing: "Glory to the newborn King."

Don't know an ANSWER? Look first in the Bible, then in the back of this book...

Jesus Our Leader

*You call me "Teacher" and "Lord." And this is right, because that is what I am. (**Jesus,** in JOHN 13:13)*

LETTER SCRAMBLE: JESUS SHOWS US HOW TO PRAY—
Unscramble the words on the right to say the "Lord's Prayer" (MATTHEW 6:9-13)

1. Our ________ in heaven — *h e r F a t*
2. hallowed be your ________ — *e n a m*
3. your ________ come, your will be done — *g o m d i n k*
4. on earth as it is in ________. — *n a v e h e*
5. Give us ________ our daily bread. — *y o t a d*
6. ________ our debts, as we also have forgiven our debtors. — *F e v r i g o*
7. And lead us not into ________ — *n a t p i m t e t o*
8. but deliver us from the ________ one. — *v l i e*

D A Y *and* N I G H T

1. On a very eventful day in the life of Christ, He rode a young donkey into Jerusalem. The people cheered Him, and spread their their cloaks and palm branches on the road before Him. Then Jesus entered the Temple and drove out the people who were buying and selling there. That night He left the city and went to stay at a nearby village which was the home of Mary, Martha, and Lazarus. What was the name of this village? (MATTHEW 21:1-17)

2. In Luke 6:12-13 we read of a time when Jesus went out on a mountainside, and spent the night praying to God. What did He do when morning came?

3. This man was a Jewish leader, and He came to Jesus at night to talk with Him. When the man said that He was impressed by the miracles Jesus did, Jesus said, "I tell you the truth, no one can see the kingdom of God unless he is born again." Who was this man? (JOHN 3:1-3)

4. On the day Jesus died, in the middle of the day, darkness came over all of Israel for how many hours? (LUKE 23:44–45)

5. Who wrote these words: "The night is nearly over; the day is almost here. So let us put aside the deeds of darkness and put on the armor of light"? (ROMANS 13:12, 1:1)

The righteous are as bold as a lion. (PROVERBS 28:1)

WHO DO I SEE?

1. The walls of Jerusalem have been torn down for many years, but now I see someone who is putting the people to work to rebuild the walls. Who is this man?

2. I see a queen who is talking to her husband, the king. She is asking for the king to help her people—God's people—because a bad man is trying to kill them! Who is she?

3. I see a man with sores all over him. He looks like he's hurting terribly! But he isn't turning away from God, even though Satan wants him to. Who is this man?

Find these answers in **NEHEMIAH 1—3**, **ESTHER 1—10**, and **JOB 1, 42.**

4. Through an open window in his room, I hear a man praying to God, even though the king of Babylon and his men have ordered that no one can pray to anyone except the king. What is the name of the man who is praying?

5. I hear a man who is telling the king of Babylon about a dream which the king had. Who is this man who can tell so much about dreams?

6. I hear the sound of crashing waves, and the wind blowing hard. And on a ship on the stormy sea, I hear a man telling the sailors on the ship that he has been running away from God. Who is this man?

7. I hear the sound of the king's voice at the Temple in Jerusalem. All the people have gathered together, and the king is reading to them from a scroll. It's a scroll of the Scriptures, and it has been lost for many years. But now it has been found, and this king is glad, because he loves God's Word. Who is he?

Find these answers in **Daniel 6**; **Daniel 2**; **Jonah 1**; and **2 Chronicles 34**.

All Your Heart

Love the Lord your God with all your heart…
*(**Jesus,** in Matthew 22:37)*

1. God said to this king, "Ask for whatever you want me to give you." So this king asked God to give him a heart of wisdom — and God did just that. Who was this king? (1 Kings 3:4-12)

▼▼▼

Place the words at the bottom of the page in the right places in this passage (Romans 10:9):

"If you confess with your mouth, (2) '______ is Lord,' and believe in your (3) ______ that God raised him from the (4) ______ you will be (5) ______ ."

heart *dead* *saved* *Jesus*

Love the Lord your God...with all your mind...
*(**Jesus,** in MATTHEW 22:37)*

UNLOCK THE TREASURE BOX:

What's the KEY WORD *(it goes where you see the ***)* in this passage?

____
* * *

(It begins with the letter "M")

"Those who live according to the sinful nature have their ***s set on what that nature desires; but those who live in accordance with the Spirit have their ***s set on what the Spirit desires. The *** of sinful man is death, but the *** controlled by the Spirit is life and peace."

— ROMANS 8:5-6

Don't know an ANSWER? Look first in the Bible, then in the back of this book...

Jesus Our King

He is Lord of lords and King of kings—and with him will be his called, chosen and faithful followers. (REVELATION 17:14)

Jesus told a story about two men who built houses (MATTHEW 7:24–27). When a stormy flood came, one man's house fell down with a crash, because it was built on sand.

1. The other man's house stood strong. What was it built on?
2. Jesus said that *we* are like the man who built his house on sand when we do what?
3. Jesus said that *we* are like the other man—the man whose house did not fall in the storm—when we do what?

♥ Which of these two builders are *you* most like?

EXTRA EXERCISE—*Keep your Bible handy!*

GREAT STARTS — These verses are all the OPENING LINES in a book of the Bible. Name the book each verse is from.

1. In the beginning, God created the heavens and the earth.
2. In the beginning was the Word, and the Word was with God, and the Word was God.
3. Blessed is the man who does not walk in the counsel of the wicked.
4. In the land of Uz there lived a man whose name was Job.
5. After the death of Moses the servant of the Lord, the Lord said to Joshua son of Nun, Moses' aide: "Moses my servant is dead."
6. The revelation of Jesus Christ, which God gave him to show his servants what must soon take place.
7. The oracle that Habakkuk the prophet received: "How long, O Lord, must I call for help, but you do not listen?"
8. The words of Amos, one of the shepherds of Tekoa—what he saw concerning Israel two years before the earthquake.

God's People

You are a chosen people, a royal priesthood, a holy nation, a people belonging to God. (1 PETER 2:9)

WHAT'S TO EAT—OR NOT TO EAT?

1. Adam and Eve ate fruit from a tree that God told them not to eat from. What was the name of the tree? (GENESIS 2:17, 3:1–13)

2. Jacob cooked something. Then his brother Esau came back from hunting, and he was hungry. He wanted some of Jacob's food. He wanted some so badly that he traded his birthright for it. What is it that Jacob made? (GENESIS 25:27–34)

3. Three visitors dropped in unexpectedly to see Abraham and Sarah. Abraham and Sarah quickly prepared bread, beef, curds and milk for them. The visitors had a message for Abraham and Sarah. What was it? (GENESIS 18:1–10)

4. Pharaoh, king of Egypt, had a dream that Joseph was later able to explain to him. In Pharaoh's dream, seven animals which were skinny and ugly ate up seven which were pretty and fat. What kind of animals were these? (GENESIS 41)

5. The people of Israel roasted meat to celebrate the Passover — the night when God brought death to the oldest son in each Egyptian family, but not the families of Israel. What kind of meat did God tell them to roast? (EXODUS 12:1–4)

6. For celebrating Passover, the people of Israel also ate bread with one ingredient left out. Which ingredient was that? (GENESIS 12:8)

7. The people of Israel left Egypt, and wandered for forty years in the desert. Each night while they were there, God sent them food from heaven. It was white flakes of bread that had a taste like honey. What was it called? (EXODUS 16)

8. God was taking good care of the people of Israel in the desert. But some of them got tired of manna, and wanted meat to eat. So one day God sent them meat. What kind of meat did He send them? (NUMBERS 11)

♥ What does it mean to you to be a part of God's people?

Don't know an ANSWER? Look first in the Bible, then in the back of this book...

Then the Lord said, "This is the land I promised on oath to Abraham, Isaac and Jacob." (DEUTERONOMY 34:4)

THE PROMISE—Who did God make each of these promises to? *(Clue: All three names are found in the verse above.)*

1. "The whole land of Canaan, where you are now an alien, I will give as an everlasting possession to you and your descendants after you, and I will be their God" (GENESIS 17:3-8).

2. "To you and your descendants I will give all these lands and will confirm the oath I swore to your father Abraham" (GENESIS 26:2-3).

3. "I am the Lord, the God of Abraham and the God of Isaac. I will give you and your descendants the land on which you are lying" (GENESIS 28:10-13).

WHICH WAY?—
If you were starting a trip from Jerusalem back in Bible times, which direction would you go to get to these places? Match each place name to an arrow on the map.

PLACES: *Great Sea (Mediterranean)* *Dead Sea* *Sea of Galilee* *Jordan River* *Mount of Olives*

1. ____________

2. ____________

JERUSALEM

5. ____________ ★ 3. ____________

4. ____________

Talking with God

Ask and it will be given to you; seek and you will find; knock and the door will be opened to you. (***Jesus,*** *in* MATTHEW *7:7)*

FAMOUS PRAYERS IN THE BIBLE—Tell who prayed each one of these prayers:

1. "My Father, if it is possible, may this cup be taken from me. Yet not as I will, but as you will" (**MATTHEW 26:39**).
2. "Lord Jesus, receive my spirit.... Lord, do not hold this sin against them" (**ACTS 7:59-60**).
3. "Create in me a pure heart, O God, and renew a steadfast spirit within me. Do not cast me from your presence or take your Holy Spirit from me. Restore to me the joy of your salvation and grant me a willing spirit, to sustain me" (**PSALM 51:10-12**).

4. "O Sovereign Lord, remember me. O God, please strengthen me just once more, and let me with one blow get revenge on the Philistines for my two eyes" (Judges 16:28).

5. "O Lord, why should your anger burn against your people, whom you brought out of Egypt with great power and a mighty hand? Why should the Egyptians say, 'It was with evil intent that he brought them out, to kill them in the mountains and to wipe them off the face of the earth'? Turn from your fierce anger; relent and do not bring disaster on your people" (Exodus 32:11-13).

6. "O God of my father Abraham, God of my father Isaac, O Lord, who said to me, 'Go back to your country and your relatives, and I will make you prosper,' I am unworthy of all the kindness and faithfulness you have shown your servant. I had only my staff when I crossed this Jordan, but now I have become two groups. Save me, I pray, from the hand of my brother Esau" (Genesis 32:9–12).

7. "Now my eyes have seen you. Therefore I despise myself and repent in dust and ashes" (Job 42:5-6).

8. "O Lord Almighty, if you will only look upon your servant's misery and remember me, and not forget your servant but give her a son, then I will give him to the Lord for all the days of his life, and no razor will ever be used on his head" (1 Samuel 1:10-11).

The Way of Wisdom

Honey from the comb is sweet to your taste.
Know also that wisdom is sweet to your soul. (PROVERBS 24:13-14)

ABC's—Words that start with each letter of the alphabet will complete these verses from **PROVERBS**, the wisdom book. Use the clue that follows each letter to find the missing word.

A— (CLUE:) *Tiny insects that crawl on the ground and build little hills for their homes;* (VERSE:) "A__________ are not very strong. But they store up food in the summer" **(30:25)**.

B— *A large, furry animal that can stand on its hind legs;* "It is better to meet a b________ robbed of her cubs than to meet a foolish person doing foolish things" **(17:12)**.

C— *A young son or daughter;* "Train a c__________ how to live the right way. Then even when he is old, he will still live that way" **(22:6)**.

D—*Something built to hold back water in a river;* "Starting a quarrel is like a leak in a d________. So stop the quarrel before a fight breaks out" **(17:14)**.

E— *(This one has two different words, and the clues are in the verse.)* "The Lord has made both these things: E_______ that can hear and e________ that can see" **(20:12)**.

F— *A thing or place in which heat is made;* "A hot f__________ tests silver and gold. In the same way, the Lord tests a person's heart" **(17:3)**.

G—*A color between white and black;* "G________ hair is like a crown of honor. You earn it by living a good life" **(16:31)**.

H—*Joyful, glad; not sad;* "Those who always respect the Lord will be h____________" **(28:14)**.

I— *A useful metal from which many tools are made;* "I_______ can sharpen i_______. In the same way, people can help each other" **(27:17)**.

J— *To decide what is right and fair;* "A king sits on his throne and j__________ people. He knows evil when he sees it" **(20:8)**.

CONTINUED ON NEXT PAGE

K— *To be certain in your mind;* "Don't brag about what will happen tomorrow. You don't really k______ what will happen then" (27:1).

L— *A strong, fierce animal, the largest kind of cat;* "A lazy person says, 'There's a l______ outside! I might get killed out in the street!'" (22:13).

M—*What you take to help you get well;* "A happy heart is like good m__________. But a broken spirit drains your strength" (17:22).

N—*What holds up your head;* "Keep your father's commands. Don't forget your mother's teaching. Remember their words forever. Let it be as if they were tied around your n________" (6:20-21).

O—*Not in;* "A person who is careful about what he says keeps himself o______ of trouble" (21:23).

P— *What you say to God;* "The Lord does not listen to the wicked. But he hears the p________ of those who do right" (15:29).

Q—*Fast;* "If you act too q__________, you might make a mistake" (19:2).

R— *Not wrong;* "People enjoy giving good answers! Saying the r________ word at the r________ time is so pleasing!" (15:23).

S— *To make music with your voice;* "An evil person is trapped by his own sin. But a good person can s________ and be happy" (29:6).

T— *What you bite with, and sound some letters with;* "Some people have t________ like swords. It is as if their jaws are full of knives. They want to remove the poor people from the earth. They want to get rid of the needy" (30:14).

U— *Not down;* "How long will you lie there, you lazy person? When will you get u__ from sleeping?" (6:9).

V— *Foods such as tomatoes, potatoes, cucumbers, cabbage, and so on;* "It is better to eat v____________ with those who love you than to eat meat with those who hate you" (15:17).

W— *Rich;* "It is better to be poor and respect the Lord than to be w_________ and have much trouble" (15:16).

X— *A big farm animal used to pull plows and wagons (the "x" is at the end of the word);* "With the strength of an __x much grain can be grown" (14:4).

Y and Z— *Not being willing to work hard (the "z" and "y" are at the end of the word);* "The ____zy person is like a door that turns back and forth on its hinges. He stays in bed and turns over and over" (26:14).

Holy Spirit

"The Holy Spirit...will teach you all things and will remind you of everything I have said to you." (**Jesus,** in JOHN 14:26)

1. After Jesus was baptized, the Holy Spirit came upon Jesus, coming down from heaven like a ___________. (LUKE 3:22)

▼ ▼ ▼

In Acts 2:1-12, when the Holy Spirit came and filled the followers of Jesus...

2. What strange sound did they hear?
3. What strange sight did they see?
4. In what new ways did they speak?
5. And what did they say?

The Way of Love

Love never fails. (1 Corinthians 13:8)

SWORD-SHARPENERS—"The sword of the Spirit…is the word of God" (**Ephesians 6:17**). For each verse below, fill in the right word at the beginning — at the "tip of the sword." (When you read down, the first letters of these words will spell the word LOVE.)

"L________ after him, and when I return I will reimburse you for any extra expense you may have" (**Luke 10:35**).

"O________ man gives freely, yet gains even more" (**Proverbs 11:24**).

"V________ rarely will anyone die for a righteous man, though for a good man someone might possibly dare to die. But God demonstrates his own love for us in this: While we were still sinners, Christ died for us" (**Romans 5:7-8**).

"E________ 'sinners' love those who love them" (**Luke 6:32**).

Don't know an ANSWER? Look first in the Bible, then in the back of this book…

And God said, "Let there be lights in the expanse of the sky to separate the day from the night, and let them serve as signs to mark seasons and days and years." (Genesis 1:14)

TIME LINE: Match the following events with the approximate date shown beside the time line on the next page.

1. David picks five smooth stones from a stream; he'll use just one to kill Goliath. (1 Samuel 17)
2. The curtain of the Temple is torn in two when Jesus is crucified in Jerusalem. (Luke 23:44-46)
3. God tells Abram (who is later called Abraham) to leave his country and his father and go to the land that God will show him. (Genesis 12:1)

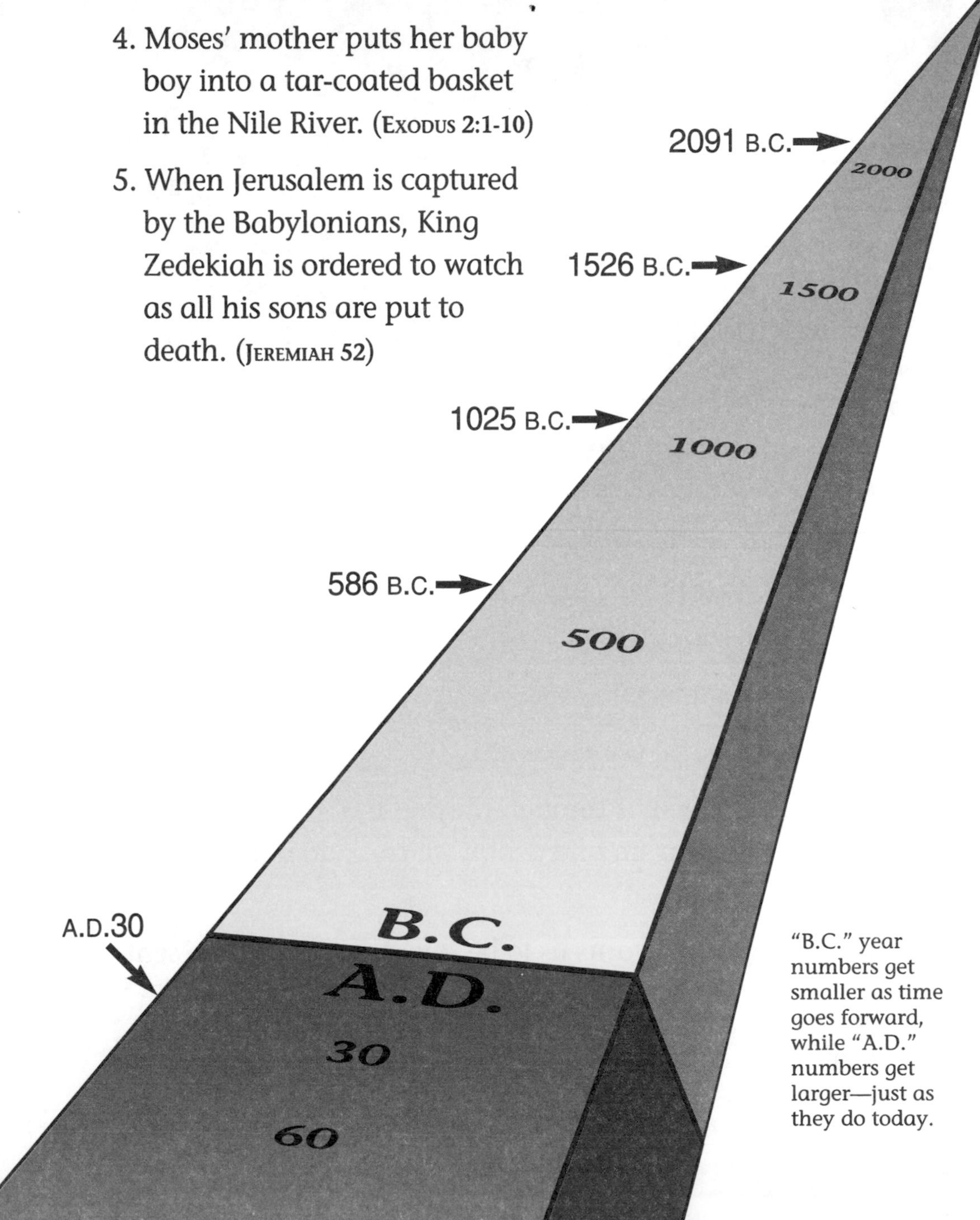
4. Moses' mother puts her baby boy into a tar-coated basket in the Nile River. (Exodus 2:1-10)
5. When Jerusalem is captured by the Babylonians, King Zedekiah is ordered to watch as all his sons are put to death. (Jeremiah 52)
2091 B.C.
2000
1526 B.C.
1500
1025 B.C.
1000
586 B.C.
500
A.D.30
B.C.
A.D.
30
60
"B.C." year numbers get smaller as time goes forward, while "A.D." numbers get larger—just as they do today.

Jesus lives forever.... He is always able to save those who come to God through him. (HEBREWS 7:24-25)

TRUE OR FALSE: WHY DID JESUS HAVE TO DIE? —Answer True or False for each statement:

1. All of us are sinners. (see ROMANS 3:23)
2. Sin leads to death. (see ROMANS 6:23)
3. Unless God helped us through the death of Christ, we could not be saved from sin and death; we can't do it on our own. (see ROMANS 5:6, 5:14, 4:25)
4. God loves us, and wants us to be saved; that's why He sent His Son Jesus to die for us. (see ROMANS 5:8)

♥ What questions might be in *your* mind about why Jesus had to die?

SCRIPTURE SCRAMBLE—JESUS SPEAKS FROM THE CROSS: Rearrange the words correctly to hear what Christ said while dying on the cross:

5. *forgive Father, them,*
they for do know not
they are what doing.

LUKE 23:34

6. *you tell I the truth,*
in paradise. today will be with me you

LUKE 23:43

7. *your here Dear is woman, son....*

JOHN 19:26

8. *your Here is mother.*

JOHN 19:27

9. *my God, God, My*
forsaken have why you me?

MATTHEW 27:46

10. *I thirsty. am*

JOHN 19:28

11. *is finished. It*

JOHN 19:30

12. *your into Father, hands*
my commit I spirit.

LUKE 23:46

Don't know an ANSWER? Look first in the Bible, then in the back of this book...

Soldiers and Kings

Praise be to the Lord my Rock, who trains my hands for war, my fingers for battle. (PSALM 144:1)

1. Joshua marched his army around this city one time each day for six days. The next day they marched around the city seven times. The priests blew their trumpets and the people shouted. Then the walls came falling down, and Israel captured the city. What city was this? (JOSHUA 6)
2. This man first found out that he was going to be Israel's king when he went to look for some lost donkeys. Who was he? (1 SAMUEL 9—10)
3. This king of Israel had seven older brothers, but none of them got to be king. Who was he? (1 SAMUEL 16)

4. This king wrote many songs about his love for God. One of his songs begins like this: "The Lord is my shepherd; I shall not be in want. He makes me lie down in green pastures..." Who was this king? (Psalm 23)

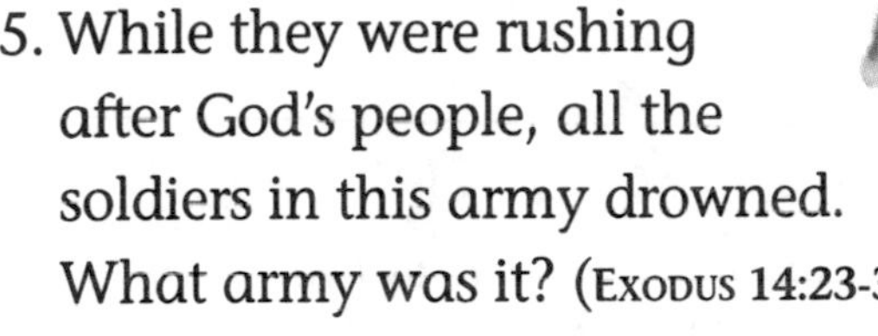

5. While they were rushing after God's people, all the soldiers in this army drowned. What army was it? (Exodus 14:23-31)

6. This king was the wisest man in the world. Who was he? (1 Kings 4:31)

7. This mean king ruled Israel in the days of the prophet Elijah. He married the evil woman Jezebel, and he worshiped the false god Baal instead of worshiping God. Who was he? (*Clue: His name rhymes with "crab"*—1 Kings 16:29-33)

8. He was only eight years old when he became king. He was a good king, and he got workers to repair the Temple in Jerusalem. (2 Kings 22)

9. This king of Babylon had a dream, and only Daniel the Hebrew could explain the meaning of it. Who was this king? (Daniel 4)

Coming Kingdom

I will not drink of this fruit of the vine again until that day when I drink it new with you in my Father's kingdom. (**Jesus,** *in* MATTHEW *26:29*)

THE GREATEST KING—

1. In Revelation 19:16, we read that when Jesus comes back to earth, He will have a mighty title written on his robe and on his thigh. Give the missing words in this title: "K______ OF KINGS AND L______ OF LORDS."

▼▼▼

Place the words at the bottom of the page in the right places in this passage (REVELATION 11:15):

"The (2) ______ of the world has (3) ______ the kingdom of our Lord and of His (4) ______, and he will reign for (5) ______ and ever."

Christ ever become kingdom

I remind you to fan into flame the gift of God which is in you.
(2 Timothy 1:6)

UNLOCK THE TREASURE BOX:

What's the KEY WORD *(it goes where you see the* ***) in this passage?

______
* * *

(It begins with the letter "S")

Then he turned to the disciples and said privately, "Blessed are the eyes that *** what you ***. For I tell you that many prophets and kings wanted to *** what you *** but did not *** it, and to hear what you hear but did not hear it."

— **Jesus, in Luke 10:23-24**

Don't know an ANSWER? Look first in the Bible, then in the back of this book...

The Great Battle

Our fight is not against people on earth.... We are fighting against the spiritual powers of evil in the heavenly world. (EPHESIANS 6:12)

UNLOCK THE TREASURE BOX:

What's the KEY WORD *(it goes where you see the ***)* that's used throughout this passage?

____

* * *

(It begins with the letter "S")

"Put on the full armor of God so that you can take your *** against the devil's schemes.... Therefore put on the full armor of God, so that when the day of evil comes, you may be able to *** your ground, and after you have done everything, to *** . *** firm then..."

—EPHESIANS 6:11-14

LIARS IN THE BIBLE—Who made each of these dishonest statements:

1. "I am Esau your firstborn. I have done as you told me. Please sit up and eat some of my game so that you may give me your blessing" (Genesis 27:19).
2. "You will not surely die. For God knows that when you eat of it your eyes will be opened, and you will be like God, knowing good and evil" (Genesis 3:4-5).
3. "I don't know this man you're talking about" (Mark 14:71).
4. "I did not laugh" (Genesis 18:15).
5. "If anyone ties me with seven fresh thongs that have not been dried, I'll become as weak as any other man" (Judges 16:7-13).
6. "Go and make a careful search for the child. As soon as you find him, report to me, so that I too may go and worship him" (Matthew 2:8).
7. "I have carried out the Lord's instructions" (1 Samuel 15:13).

▼ ▼ ▼

In Acts 5:1-11 we read of a husband and wife who sold some property in order to give the money to the church, but who secretly kept back some of the money for themselves.

8. What were the names of this man and woman?
9. What happened to them?

Don't know an ANSWER? Look first in the Bible, then in the back of this book...

Treasure Chest

Store up for yourselves treasures in heaven, where moth and rust do not destroy, and where thieves do not break in and steal.
*(**Jesus,** in MATTHEW 6:20)*

POWER PASSAGE—Here's the passage (**MATTHEW 6:19-20**) from which the verse above is taken. Complete it here by adding the right words in the right places. Choose them from the list of words at the bottom of the page (not all of them will be used).

"Do not (1) ______ up for yourselves (2) ______ on earth, where (3) ______ and rust destroy, and where (4) ______ break in and steal. But store up for yourselves treasures in heaven, where moth and rust do not destroy, and where thieves do not break in and steal. For where (5) ______ treasure is, there your (6) ______ will be also"

thieves rich treasures steal your store years heart moth

SWORD-SHARPENERS—"The sword of the Spirit…is the word of God" (EPHESIANS 6:17). For each verse below, fill in the right word at the beginning — at the "tip of the sword." (When you read down, the first letters of these words will spell the word TREASURE.)

"T________ and see that the Lord is good; blessed is the man who takes refuge in him" (PSALM 34:8).

"R________ Jesus Christ, raised from the dead, descended from David. This is my gospel, for which I am suffering even to the point of being chained like a criminal" (2 TIMOTHY 2:8-9).

"E________ valley shall be raised up, every mountain and hill made low; the rough ground shall become level, the rugged places a plain" (ISAIAH 40:4-5).

"A________ your words are true; all your righteous laws are eternal" (PSALM 119:160).

"S________, success to you, and success to those who help you, for your God will help you" (1 CHRONICLES 12:18).

"U________ then, that those who believe are children of Abraham" (GALATIANS 3:7).

"R________ down your hand from on high; deliver me and rescue me from the mighty waters" (PSALM 144:7).

"E________ one another daily, as long as it is called Today, so that none of you may be hardened by sin's deceitfulness" (HEBREWS 3:13).

Don't know an ANSWER? Look first in the Bible, then in the back of this book…

★★2

Faces and Places

The Sovereign Lord will wipe away the tears from all faces.
(Isaiah 25:8)

RHYME TIME—Use these rhyme clues to tell the names of the people in this famous Old Testament family:

1. The mother's name rhymes with *sleeve.*
2. The oldest son's name rhymes with *rain.*
3. The second son's name rhymes with *table.*
4. The third son's name rhymes with *breath.*
5. The father's name rhymes with *madam.*

(Genesis 4:1-2, 4:25)

6. During a battle, this person was riding his mule and passed under an oak tree with low, thick branches. His hair got caught in the branches. The mule kept going, leaving the man hanging there. Who was he? (2 Samuel 18:1–18)

7. This person was living near the great trees of Mamre when he received word that his nephew Lot (and many other people) had been captured in a battle between nine kings. This man called out his 318 men. They attacked at night, and rescued Lot and many others. (Genesis 14:8-16)

8. God gave laws to Israel, and included in those laws were rules for going to war. In those war rules was a rule about trees. When the people went to war, and they were attacking an enemy city, God told them not to cut down a certain kind of tree. What kind of trees were these? *(Clue: It has to do with something you can eat;* Deuteronomy 20:19-20)

9. In Jerusalem, Jesus cursed a tree that did not have fruit on it when it should have. The tree immediately wilted. What kind of tree was it? (Matthew 21:18-19)

10. What kind of tree did Zacchaeus climb? (Luke 19:1-4)

11. THE TREATY TREE: After he made a treaty at Beersheba with the rulers of the nations around him, Abraham planted a tree there. What kind of tree was it? (Genesis 21:33)

Don't know an ANSWER? Look first in the Bible, then in the back of this book…

Jesus Our Friend

I have called you friends, for everything that I learned from my Father I have made known to you. (***Jesus****, in* JOHN *15:15*)

1. In Hebrews 2:11-12, we read that those who have been made holy through the blood of Christ are now *of the same family* with Jesus, the One who makes them holy. Therefore, the passage goes on, "Jesus is not ashamed to call them ____________." *(Clue: the word starts with "B", and you can't be one with someone unless you and he are part of the same family.)*

2. Jesus said, "I no longer call you servants, because a servant does not know his master's business." Instead, Jesus said, He was calling them something else. What was it? (JOHN 15:15)

SCRIPTURE SCRAMBLE: STORIES JESUS TOLD— Rearrange the words in each numbered sentence below to hear a line from one of the parables Jesus told.

3. *celebrate We to be and glad had*
dead yours because this brother of was
alive and is again;
lost he was and is found.
LUKE 15:32

4. *me; Rejoice with*
lost I sheep. found my have
LUKE 15:6

5. *me; with Rejoice*
found have my coin. I lost
LUKE 15:9

6. *farmer out sow to his went seed. A*
MATTHEW 13:3

7. *down going A was man*
Jericho, from to Jerusalem
robbers. hands when he into the of fell
LUKE 10:30

8. *look would even not up He to heaven,*
beat breast and but said, his
sinner." have on mercy "God, me, a
LUKE 18:13

Don't know an ANSWER? Look first in the Bible, then in the back of this book...

Bible Heroes

They were brave warriors, ready for battle... Their faces were the faces of lions...they were as swift as gazelles in the mountains. (1 CHRONICLES 12:8)

WORK TIME: Who did each of these jobs?

1. Writing down the right name to give to Elizabeth's new baby boy. (He wrote, "His name is John"— LUKE 1:57-66.)
2. Telling Mary that she was going to have a baby who would be God's Son. (LUKE 1:26-38)
3. Wrapping the baby Jesus up in cloths, to keep Him warm. (LUKE 2:5–7)
4. Following a star to find Jesus, the newborn King, so they could worship Him. (MATTHEW 2:1-12)
5. Taking the child Jesus and His mother to Egypt so King Herod would not kill Him. (MATTHEW 2:13–18)

6. Bringing Jesus and His mother back to Israel from Egypt after King Herod had died. (MATTHEW 2:19–23)
7. Baptizing Jesus in the Jordan River. (MATTHEW 3:13–17)
8. Gathering up the leftovers after Jesus fed fish and bread to five thousand people. (MATTHEW 14:14–21)
9. Catching a fish that had a coin in its mouth. (MATTHEW 17:24–27)
10. Helping a man who had been terribly beaten by robbers. (LUKE 10:25–37)
11. Paying back lots of money to everyone he had cheated while working as a tax collector. (LUKE 19:1–10)
12. Taking down the body of Jesus from the cross, and putting it in a tomb. (MATTHEW 27:57–61)
13. Finding Saul, who had become blind, and touching him so that he could see again. (ACTS 9:10–19)
14. Telling a jailer in Philippi how he could be saved, after an earthquake shook the jail and caused all the doors to the jail cells to open. (ACTS 16:25–34)
15. Writing down what he saw in a wonderful dream, while he was on the island of Patmos. (REVELATION 1:9–20)

ONE-WORD CLUES—Use these groups of one-word clues to help you discover the names of Bible heroes — one name for each group of clues.

1. WISEST • BUILD • TEMPLE (1 Kings 1—8)
2. RAVENS • DROUGHT • AHAB • CARMEL • RAIN • CHARIOTS • FIRE (1 Kings 17—2 Kings 2)
3. MANTLE • JARS • OIL • AXHEAD • ROOM (2 Kings 2—6)
4. BOY • KING • REPAIR • TEMPLE • FIND • SCROLL (2 Kings 22—23)
5. THREE • VEGETABLES • BOW • FURNACE • FOUR • ALIVE (Daniel 1—3)
6. BELIEVE • ANGEL • SPIRIT • VIRGIN • CHILD • (Luke 1—2)
7. BELIEVE • ANGEL • DREAM • BETHLEHEM • EGYPT • NAZARETH (Matthew 1—2)
8. DESERT • LOCUSTS • HONEY • REPENT • BAPTIZE (Luke 3)
9. FISH • FOLLOW • DENY • ROOSTER • FEED • LAMBS (John 21:15-19; 18:25-27)
10. THREATS • DAMASCUS • ANTIOCH • MISSIONARY • ROME (Acts 26)
11. THUNDER • LOVE • PATMOS • VISION (Revelation 1:9)

The Lord is faithful to all his promises. (PSALM 145:13)

PROMISE POWER—Match the right ending *(from the list below)* to each of these powerful promises in God's Word.

1. I tell you the truth, whoever hears my word and believes him who sent me…
2. Even though I walk through the valley of the shadow of death, I will fear no evil…
3. You may ask me for anything in my name…

(A)• *for you are with me* (PSALM 27:4).

(B)• *and I will do it* (Jesus, in JOHN 14:14).

(C)• *has eternal life and will not be condemned; he has crossed over from death to life* (Jesus, in JOHN 5:24).

Bible Miracles

I will remember the deeds of the Lord; yes, I will remember your miracles of long ago. (PSALM 77:11)

1. On the first day of creation, God created light. Then He separated the light from the darkness. What name did He give to the light? (GENESIS 1:3–5)

2. What name did He give to the darkness? (GENESIS 1:3–5)

3. At the end of the first week, after God had created everything, how did He think it all looked? (GENESIS 1:31)

Unscramble the following groups of words to form the three parts of GENESIS 1:27, a great verse about how God created people:

4. *created man God in his So image; own*

5. *image him, he in the of God created*

6. *them. created male and he female*

A MIRACLE FOR PETER:

7. Jesus was standing by the Sea of Galilee one day (LUKE 5:1–11). People were crowding around Him, listening to God's Word. Then Jesus got into something that belonged to Simon Peter. What was it?

8. After Jesus finished speaking, what did He ask Peter to do?

9. Peter did what Jesus told him to, but what did he say first?

10. What happened after Peter obeyed Jesus?

11. After all this happened, what did Peter say to Jesus?

12. And how did Jesus answer Peter?

♥ What does this story tell you about Jesus?

We will not fear even if the oceans roar and foam, or if the mountains shake at the raging sea.... God says, "Be quiet and know that I am God." (PSALM 46:3-10)

MOSES GETS TO KNOW GOD:

1. Moses saw a burning bush, and went closer to see why the bush didn't burn up. Then he heard the voice of God calling his name from the bush. When Moses answered, "Here I am," what did God tell him next? (EXODUS 3:5)
2. God then told Moses that He was the God of three men. Who were those three men? (EXODUS 3:6)
3. God told Moses to go and bring the Israelites out of Egypt. Why did God say He wanted to rescue them? (EXODUS 3:7)
4. When Moses said, "Who am I, that I should do this?", God quickly said that someone would be with him. Who was it? (EXODUS 3:12)

4. Moses said, "Suppose I go to the Israelites and say to them, 'The God of your fathers has sent me to you,' and they ask me, 'What is his name?' Then what shall I tell them?" God then told Moses His name. What is it? (Exodus 3:14)

▼ ▼ ▼

LETTER SCRAMBLE—Moses was always wanting to know more about God. After He led the Israelites out of Egypt, he said to the Lord, "If you are pleased with me, teach me your ways so I may know you and continue to find favor with you." He also said to God, "Now show me your glory" (Exodus 33:12-23). Unscramble the words below to fill in the blanks and complete the answer God gave to Moses:

5. "I will cause all my ________ to pass in — *d o n g s e s o*
6. front of you, and I will proclaim my ________, — *e n a m*
7. the Lord, in your ________. I will have — *e s n e c e r p*
8. ________ on whom I will have mercy, and I will — *r y c e m*
9. have ________ on whom I will have — *s a p s o n i m o c*
10. compassion. But you cannot see my ________, — *c e f a*

for no one may see me and live."

♥ What does the Lord's name—the name He told to Moses—mean to you?

Don't know an ANSWER? Look first in the Bible, then in the back of this book...

Born Again

I tell you the truth, no one can see the kingdom of God unless he is born again. (**Jesus**, in JOHN 3:3)

PLANT THE SEEDS—"The seed is the word of God," Jesus said (LUKE 8:11). In each planter-pot, plant the right "seed-word"—the word that makes the verse complete, ready to grow in your heart.

SEED-WORDS: *Spirit forgive everything mouth becoming power God living*

1. ______________
So you must change your hearts and lives! Come back to God, and he will _______ your sins. Then the Lord will give you times of spiritual rest.
(ACTS 3:19-20)

2. ______________
He put a new song in my _______. It was a song of praise to our God. Many people will see this and worship him. Then they will trust in God.
(PSALM 40:3)

3. ______________
We were buried with him so that we could live a new life, just as Christ was raised from death by the wonderful _______ of the Father.
(Romans 6:4)

4. ______________
So now we serve God in a new way, not in the old way with written rules. Now we serve God in the new way, with the ________.
(Romans 7:6)

5. ______________
You were taught to become a new person. That new person is made to be like _____—made to be truly good and holy.
(Ephesians 4:24)

6. ______________
God has great mercy, and because of his mercy he gave us a new life. He gave us a ______ hope because Jesus Christ rose from death.
(1 Peter 1:3)

7. ______________
You have begun to live the new life. In your new life you are being made new. You are __________ like the One who made you.
(Colossians 3:10)

8. ______________
If anyone belongs to Christ, then he is made new. The old things have gone; _____________ is made new!
(2 Corinthians 5:17)

Don't know an ANSWER? Look first in the Bible, then in the back of this book...

Be Strong in the Lord

The name of the Lord is a strong tower; the righteous run to it and are safe. (PROVERBS 18:10)

UNLOCK THE TREASURE BOX:

What's the KEY WORD *(it goes where you see the ***)* in this passage?

____

* * *

(It begins with the letter "G")

"By the *** of God I am what I am, and his *** to me was not without effect. No, I worked harder than all of them — yet not I, but the *** of God that was with me."

— **PAUL, IN 1 CORINTHIANS 15:10**

BLESSINGS FOR EVERYONE

SCRIPTURE SCRAMBLE: Rearrange the words in each numbered sentence below so the blessings read correctly.

1. *Lord The you bless*
keep and you;
face the Lord make his upon you shine
you; and to gracious be
turn the Lord his toward you face
give and you peace.

(the blessing from Israel's priests, **Numbers 6:24-26**)

2. *city You be will in the blessed*
country... and blessed the in
come You will be blessed you in when
out. and you blessed when go

(God's promised blessing for Israel's obedience, **Deuteronomy 28:3-6**)

3. *nation great I will you into a make*
will and bless I you;
great, name I will your make
you and be a blessing. will
those I will who bless bless you;
curses will and you I whoever curse;
earth and all on peoples
through will be blessed you.

(God's calling of Abraham, **Genesis 12:2-3**)

Bible Numbers

How precious to me are your thoughts, O God!
How vast is the sum of them! Were I to count them,
they would outnumber the grains of sand. (*Psalm 139:17-18*)

NUMBER KNOWLEDGE—There's a correct number that goes with each item on the list that begins below. Match it with the numbers on the next page. (Each number is used only once.)

(a) *number of days in the week that God said His people could work* (Exodus 23:12)

(b) *Goliath's approximate height in feet* (1 Samuel 17:4)

(c) *number of fish it took for Jesus to feed the 5,000* (Mark 6:38)

(d) *number of loaves of bread it took to feed the 5,000* (Mark 6:38)

(e) *number of men Jesus chose for his team of disciples* (Mark 3:14)

(f) *number of times Laban changed Jacob's wages* (Genesis 31:7)

(g) *number of books in the Bible that start with the letter "O"*

(h) *number of stars bowing down to Joseph in his dream* (GENESIS 37:9)

(i) *number of Jesse's sons, including David* (1 SAMUEL 17:12)

(j) *number of Noah's sons* (GENESIS 6:10)

(k) *number of days Lazarus was in the tomb before Jesus raised him from the dead* (JOHN 11:17)

(l) *number of times Naaman dipped himself in the Jordan River to be healed of his leprosy* (2 KINGS 5:14)

1. ____ ★
2. ____ ★ ★
3. ____ ★ ★ ★
4. ____ ★ ★ ★ ★
5. ____ ★ ★ ★ ★ ★
6. ____ ★ ★ ★ ★ ★ ★
7. ____ ★ ★ ★ ★ ★ ★ ★
8. ____ ★ ★ ★ ★ ★ ★ ★ ★
9. ____ ★ ★ ★ ★ ★ ★ ★ ★ ★
10. ____ ★ ★ ★ ★ ★ ★ ★ ★ ★ ★
11. ____ ★ ★ ★ ★ ★ ★ ★ ★ ★ ★ ★
12. ____ ★ ★ ★ ★ ★ ★ ★ ★ ★ ★ ★ ★

ALTAR CALL: In 1 Kings 18:20-40, we read about Elijah, the prophet of God, meeting the prophets of the false god Baal on Mount Carmel. After the prophets of Baal could not get their god to send fire upon their altar (although they kept asking for it from morning till noon), Elijah showed them what the real GOD would do.

13. How many stones did Elijah take to build his altar?
14. How many times was water poured upon Elijah's altar?
15. When Elijah was ready for God to send fire down on the altar, how many times did he have to pray before God did it?

Some were laughed at and beaten. Others were tied and put into prison. They were killed with stones and they were cut in half. (HEBREWS 11:36-37)

SWORD-SHARPENERS—"The sword of the Spirit…is the word of God" (EPHESIANS 6:17). For each verse below, fill in the right word at the beginning — at the "tip of the sword." (When you read down, the first letters of these words will spell the word HARD.)

"H_______ and earth will pass away, but my words will never pass away" (LUKE 21:33).

"A_______ me, O Lord, out of the goodness of your love; in your great mercy turn to me" (PSALM 69:16).

"R_______ in the Lord always. I will say it again: Rejoice!" (PHILIPPIANS 4:4).

"D_______ has been swallowed up in victory. Where, O death, is your victory? Where, O death, is your sting?" (1 CORINTHIANS 15:54–55).

Don't know an ANSWER? Look first in the Bible, then in the back of this book…

Children are a gift from the Lord. (PSALM 127:3)

A GIRL REMEMBERS A PROPHET OF ISRAEL (2 KINGS 5)—

1. This young girl from Israel had been taken captive by the king of Aram. She became the servant to a woman whose husband was the commander of the king's army in Aram. What was the commander's name?
2. When this commander became sick with leprosy, the servant girl sent word to him through his wife about a prophet in Israel who could cure him. Who was the prophet?
3. What did the commander have to do to be cured?

♥ This young girl was faithful to be a witness for the Lord in the place where He had put her. Where has God put you?

★ GOLD STAR SPECIAL ★

MORE GREAT STARTS — Name the Bible book from which each of these opening verses is taken:

1. When King David was old and well advanced in years, he could not keep warm even when they put covers over him.
2. This is what happened during the time of Xerxes, the Xerxes who ruled over 127 provinces stretching from India to Cush.
3. The beginning of the gospel about Jesus Christ, the Son of God.
4. These are the names of the sons of Israel who went to Egypt with Jacob, each with his family….
5. An oracle: The word of the Lord to Israel through Malachi. "I have loved you," says the Lord. "But you ask, 'How have you loved us?'"
6. Paul, an apostle—sent not from men nor by man, but by Jesus Christ and God the Father, who raised him from the dead…
7. The words of the Teacher, son of David, king in Jerusalem.
8. Peter, an apostle of Jesus Christ, to God's elect, strangers in the world…

Many women do noble things.... A woman who respects the Lord should be praised. (PROVERBS 31:29-30)

1. David said this to her: "Praise be to the Lord, the God of Israel, who has sent you today to meet me. May you be blessed for your good judgment and for keeping me from bloodshed this day and from avenging myself with my own hands." Who was David speaking to? (1 SAMUEL 25:32-33)
2. A woman of great beauty and great courage, she prepared banquets for the king two days in a row in order to talk with him about saving the Jews. (ESTHER 5—7)
3. Each year she made her son a new little robe, and took it to him where he lived with the priests of God. (1 SAMUEL 2:18-21)

WORDS FROM WOMEN—Name the woman who spoke each of these things in the Bible:

4. "Don't urge me to leave you or to turn back from you. Where you go I will go, and where you stay I will stay. Your people will be my people and your God my God. Where you die I will die, and there I will be buried. May the Lord deal with me, be it ever so severely, if anything but death separates you and me" (Ruth 1:16-18).
5. "The serpent deceived me, and I ate" (Genesis 3:13).
6. "Tell me the secret of your great strength and how you can be tied up and subdued" (Judges 16:6).
7. "Lord, don't you care that my sister has left me to do the work by myself? Tell her to help me!" (Luke 10:40).
8. "Drink, my lord.... I'll draw water for your camels too, until they have finished drinking" (Genesis 24:18-20).
8. "As soon as the sound of your greeting reached my ears, the baby in my womb leaped for joy. Blessed is she who has believed that what the Lord has said to her will be accomplished" (Luke 1:44-45).
10. "I am the Lord's servant. May it be to me as you have said" (Luke 1:38).
11. "Peter is at the door!" (Acts 12:13-14).

Don't know an ANSWER? Look first in the Bible, then in the back of this book...

Men in the Bible

You should recognize the value of men like these.
(1 Corinthians 16:18)

DISCIPLE DRILL: For the following questions, each answer is the name of one or more of the twelve men who made up Jesus' team of disciples. (Some names are used more than once.)

1. Jesus once said to him, "Before the rooster crows today, you will deny three times that you know me." (Luke 22:34)
2. In Matthew 4:18-19, Jesus said to these two fishermen, "Come, follow me, and I will make you fishers of men."
3. This disciple was a tax collector. (Luke 5:27-28, Matthew 9:9–13)
4. This disciple wrote two of the letters in the New Testament. In our Bible they come right after the book of James.
5. Jesus told this disciple to catch a fish with a coin in its mouth — and he did! (Matthew 17:24-27)

6. He was the brother of John. (Matthew 4:21)
7. He was the brother of Peter. (Luke 6:14)
8. He was the brother of James. (Mark 1:19)
9. He was the brother of Andrew. (John 1:40)
10. After Jesus had risen from the dead, this disciple said to the others, "Unless I see the nail marks in his hands and put my finger where the nails were, and put my hand into his side, I will not believe it." (John 20:24-25)
11. One Sunday, on a lonely island, this disciple saw the wonderful vision which became our book of Revelation. (Revelation 1:9-20)
12. This disciple was in prison one night when an angel came and freed him from his chains, and led him away. (Acts 12:1–19)
13. Jesus took these three disciples with Him high upon a mountain. There He was changed before their eyes. His clothes became dazzling white, and Elijah and Moses came and talked with Him. Who were the three disciples who saw all this? (Mark 9:2–4)
14. One of these three disciples on the mountain said to Jesus, "It is good for us to be here. Let us put up three shelters — one for you, one for Moses and one for Elijah." But he didn't really know what he should be saying. Who was he? (Mark 9:5–6)
15. This disciple betrayed Jesus. (Luke 22:47-48)

Our Home in Heaven

Our homeland is in heaven, and we are waiting for our Savior, the Lord Jesus Christ, to come from heaven. (PHILIPPIANS 3:20)

UNLOCK THE TREASURE BOX:

What's the KEY WORD *(it goes where you see the ***)* in this passage?

______

* * *

(It begins with the letter "Y". Also, try putting your own name where the key word goes in this verse.)

"In my Father's house are many rooms; if it were not so, I would have told ***. I am going there to prepare a place for ***. And if I go and prepare a place for ***, I will come back and take *** to be with me that *** also may be where I am. *** know the way to the place where I am going." — Jesus, in JOHN **14:2-4**

THE VOICE OF GOD

Each of these statements was spoken by God. For each one, tell who God was speaking to.

1. "You will crawl on your belly and you will eat dust all the days of your life" (Genesis 3:14).
2. "Never again will all life be cut off by the waters of a flood; never again will there be a flood to destroy the earth" (Genesis 9:11).
3. "Do not come any closer. Take off your sandals, for the place where you are standing is holy ground" (Exodus 3:5).
4. "I will make you into a great nation and I will bless you; I will make your name great, and you will be a blessing. I will bless those who bless you, and whoever curses you I will curse; and all peoples on earth will be blessed through you" (Genesis 12:1-3).
5. "By the sweat of your brow you will eat your food until you return to the ground, since from it you were taken; for dust you are and to dust you will return" (Genesis 3:19).
6. "Make a snake and put it up on a pole; anyone who is bitten can look at it and live" (Numbers 21:8).
7. "Take your son, your only son, Isaac, whom you love, and go to the region of Moriah. Sacrifice him there as a burnt offering on one of the mountains I will tell you about" (Genesis 22:2).

These words are like nails that have been driven in firmly. They are wise teachings that come from God the Shepherd. (Ecclesiastes 12:11)

FOUR SOILS: In Luke 8:4-15, Jesus talked about four kinds of soil on which a farmer scattered seed. Here's what Jesus said about each place where the seed fell:

ROADSIDE "Some seed fell BESIDE THE ROAD. People walked on the seed, and the birds ate all this seed."

ROCKY "Some seed fell ON ROCK. It began to grow, but then died because it had no water."

THORNY "Some seed fell AMONG THORNY WEEDS. The seed grew, but later the weeds choked the good plants."

GOOD "Some seed fell ON GOOD GROUND. This seed grew and made 100 times more grain."

Jesus said each of these four kinds of soil was like a certain kind of person. For the numbered statements below, match the right soil with the kind of person Jesus said that soil is like:

1. Those who hear God's teaching with a good, honest heart. They obey God's teaching and patiently produce good fruit.
2. Those who hear God's teaching, but they let the worries, riches, and pleasures of this life keep them from growing. So they never produce good fruit.
3. People who hear God's teaching, but then the devil comes and takes it away from their hearts. So they cannot believe the teaching and be saved.
4. Those who hear God's teaching and accept it gladly. But they don't have deep roots. They believe for a while, but then trouble comes. They stop believing and turn away from God.

MUSTARD MIRACLES: In Matthew 13:31-32 (and also Mark 4:30-34), Jesus told a parable about a man and a mustard seed.

5. What did the man do with the seed?
6. What did Jesus say about the mustard seed?
7. What does the mustard seed do?

▼▼▼

8. In Matthew 17:20, Jesus said that if we have faith even as small as a mustard seed, then what can we say and do to a mountain?

Angels

This is what God said about the angels: "God makes his angels become like winds. He makes his servants become like flames of fire." (HEBREWS 1:7)

1. In this man's dream, angels were going up and down a stairway that reached to heaven. Who was the man? (**GENESIS 28:10-15**)

▼ ▼ ▼

A huge crowd of angels praised God with these words, while shepherds near Bethlehem listened (**LUKE 2:13-14**). Place the words at the bottom of the page in the right places in this passage:

(2) "________ to God in the (3) ________,
and on (4) ________ peace to men
on whom his (5) ________ rests."

highest *Glory* *favor* *earth*

Bible Commands

Loving God means obeying his commands.
And God's commands are not too hard for us. (1 JOHN 5:3)

SCRIPTURE SCRAMBLE: Rearrange the words in each numbered sentence below so that the Ten Commandments (EXODUS 20) read correctly.

The first four commandments have to do with our love for God:

I am the Lord your God, who brought you
out of Egypt, out of the land of slavery.

1. *no shall have You*
   before me. other gods

2. *make You not for shall*
   idol... yourself an

3. *not misuse shall the You*
name your God... the Lord of

4. *Sabbath Remember day the*
it holy. keeping by

▼▼▼

The last six commandments have to do with our love for one another:

5. *father your Honor*
your and mother...

6. *murder. not shall You*

7. *not commit shall adultery. You*

8. *shall You not steal.*

9. *give You testimony shall false not*
against neighbor. your

10. *You not covet... shall*

God Became a Man

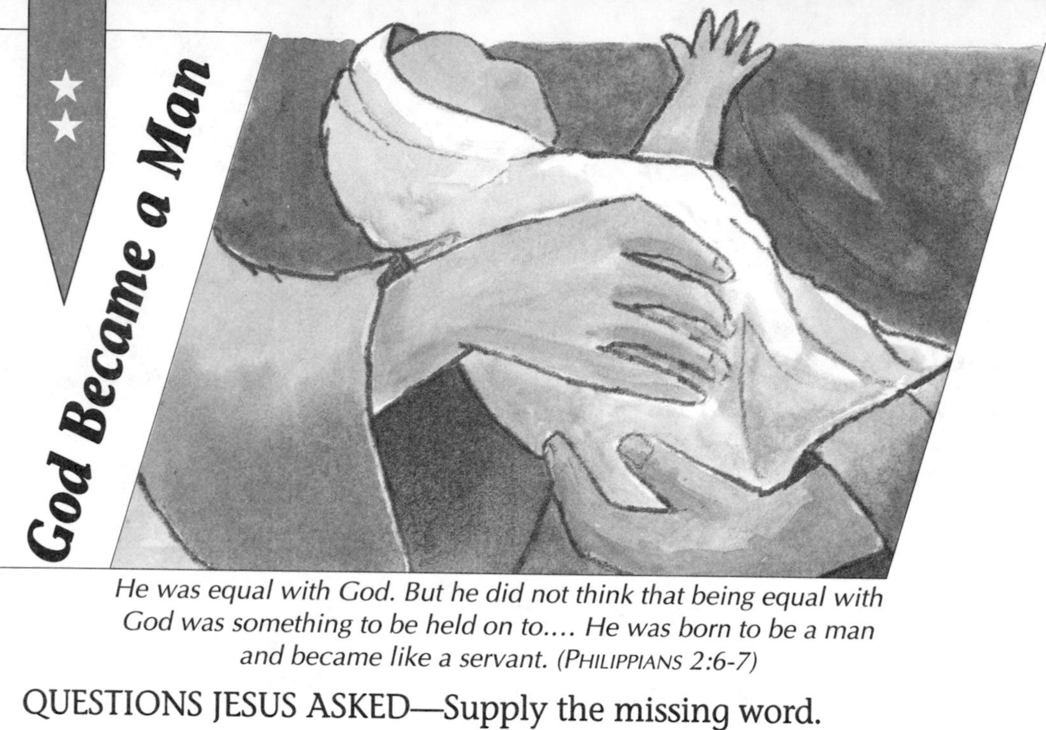

He was equal with God. But he did not think that being equal with God was something to be held on to.... He was born to be a man and became like a servant. (PHILIPPIANS 2:6-7)

QUESTIONS JESUS ASKED—Supply the missing word.

1. *To a lame man:* "Which is easier: to say, 'Your sins are f__________,' or to say, 'Get up and walk'?" (MATTHEW 9:5).
2. *To Mary and Joseph:* "Why were you searching for me? Didn't you know I had to be in my Father's h______?" (LUKE 2:49).
3. *When He healed ten lepers:* "Were not all ten cleansed? Where are the other nine? Was no one found to return and give p______ to God except this foreigner?" (LUKE 17:17-18).
4. *To the Jews:* "Why are you t______ to kill me?" (JOHN 7:19).

5. *To Nicodemus:* "You are Israel's teacher, and do you not u________ these things?" (JOHN 3:10).

6. *To a blind man:* "Do you b_______ that I am able to do this?" (MATTHEW 9:28).

7. *To some Jews in Jerusalem:* "Why are you angry with me for healing the whole man on the S___________?" (JOHN 7:23).

8. *To the Pharisees:* "What do you think about the Christ? Whose s____ is he?" (MATTHEW 22:42).

9. *To the disciples:* "What about y____? Who do y____ say I am?" (MATTHEW 16:15).

10. *To Peter:* "What do you think, Simon? From whom do the k______ of the earth collect duty and taxes—from their own sons or from others?" (MATTHEW 17:25).

11. *To Peter, James, and John:* "Could you men not keep watch with me for one h______?" (MATTHEW 26:40).

12. *To the Samaritan woman at Jacob's well:* "Will you give me a d_____?" (JOHN 4:7).

13. *To a crowd of armed men:* "Am I leading a rebellion, that you have come out with swords and clubs to c________ me?" (MATTHEW 26:55).

14. *To two disciples on the road to Emmaus:* "How foolish you are, and how s_____ of heart to believe all that the prophets have spoken! Did not the Christ have to suffer these things and then enter his glory?" (LUKE 24:25-26).

Don't know an ANSWER? Look first in the Bible, then in the back of this book...

*You call me "Teacher" and "Lord." And this is right, because that is what I am. (**Jesus,** in John 13:13)*

SCRIPTURE SCRAMBLE: STORIES JESUS TOLD— Rearrange the words in each numbered sentence below to hear a line from one of the parables Jesus told.

1.

went He him to
bandaged his and wounds,
wine. on oil and pouring
donkey, he man the on his Then own put
inn took to an him
cure and of him. took

Luke 10:34

2. *faithful Well done, and good servant!*
faithful You been have
things; a few with
charge I will you in put
things. of many
happiness. share and your Come master's

MATTHEW 25:21

3. *everyone has, I you to who that tell*
given, more will be
nothing, one but for the who has as
even he has what
taken away. be will

LUKE 19:26

4. *cattle My and fattened oxen*
butchered, have been
ready. and is everything
banquet. the Come to wedding

MATTHEW 22:4

5. *mercy Shouldn't have you had*
servant on fellow your
you? had as I on just

MATTHEW 18:33

Bold and Brave

The righteous are as bold as a lion. (PROVERBS 28:1)

UNLOCK THE
TREASURE BOX:

What's the KEY WORD *(it goes where you see the* ***) in this passage?

____

* * *

(It begins with the letter "L")

"*** has come into the world, but men loved darkness instead of *** because their deeds were evil. Everyone who does evil hates the ***, and will not come into the *** for fear that his deeds will be exposed. But whoever lives by the truth comes into the *** so that it may be seen plainly that what he has done has been done through God."
— Jesus, in JOHN 3:19-21

BRAVE WORDS—Who made each of these courageous statements?

1. "I will go to the king, even though it is against the law. And if I perish, I perish" (Esther 4:16).
2. "Choose for yourselves this day whom you will serve.... But as for me and my household, we will serve the Lord" (Joshua 24:15).
3. "We should go up and take possession of the land, for we can certainly do it" (Numbers 13:30).
4. "Judge for yourselves whether it is right in God's sight to obey you rather than God. For we cannot help speaking about what we have seen and heard" (Acts 4:19-20).
5. "Go to the hills so the pursuers will not find you. Hide yourselves there three days until they return, and then go on your way" (Joshua 2:16).
6. "Come, let's go over to the outpost of those uncircumcised fellows. Perhaps the Lord will act in our behalf. Nothing can hinder the Lord from saving, whether by many or by few" (1 Samuel 14:6).
7. "Should a man like me run away? Or should one like me go into the temple to save his life? I will not go!" (Nehemiah 6:11).

Don't know an ANSWER? Look first in the Bible, then in the back of this book...

All Your Heart

Love the Lord your God with all your heart...
*(**Jesus,** in MATTHEW 22:37)*

TRIPLE SEARCH:

How many words can you find that are included in ALL THREE of these verses?

I have sought your face with all my heart; be gracious to me according to your promise.
(PSALM 119:58)

My heart says of you, "Seek his face!" Your face, Lord, I will seek.
(PSALM 27:8)

As water reflects a face, so a man's heart reflects the man.
(PROVERBS 27:19)

Love the Lord your God...with all your mind...
*(**Jesus,** in MATTHEW 22:37)*

UNLOCK THE TREASURE BOX:

What's the KEY WORD *(it goes where you see the ***)* in this passage?

______

(It begins with the letter "T")

Jesus answered, "You are right in saying I am a king. In fact, for this reason I was born, and for this I came into the world, to testify to the ***. Everyone on the side of *** listens to me."

"What is ***?" Pilate asked.

— **JOHN 18:37-38**

He is Lord of lords and King of kings—and with him will be his called, chosen and faithful followers. (REVELATION 17:14)

SCRIPTURE SCRAMBLE: Rearrange the words in each numbered sentence below so that these "kingdom sayings" of Jesus read correctly.

1. *kingdom gospel of This the world preached whole will be the in nations, a testimony as to all end come. and the will then*

   MATTHEW 24:14

2. *sun shine The will like the righteous kingdom Father. their of in the*

   MATTHEW 13:43

EXTRA EXERCISE—***Keep your Bible handy!***

EXCITING ENDINGS — Name the book that ends with each of these verses:

1. He who testifies to these things says, "Yes, I am coming soon." Amen. Come, Lord Jesus. The grace of the Lord Jesus be with God's people. Amen.
2. And they will go out and look upon the dead bodies of those who rebelled against me; their worm will not die, nor will their fire be quenched, and they will be loathsome to all mankind.
3. David built an altar to the Lord there and sacrificed burnt offerings and fellowship offerings. Then the Lord answered prayer in behalf of the land, and the plague on Israel was stopped.
4. As for you, go your way till the end. You will rest, and then at the end of the days you will rise to receive your allotted inheritance.
5. *(Two books end the same, with only a slight difference in wording. Which two books end with these words:)* So Jehoiachin put aside his prison clothes and for the rest of his life ate regularly at the king's table. Day by day the king of Babylon gave Jehoiachin a regular allowance as long as he lived, till the day of his death.

God's People

You are a chosen people, a royal priesthood, a holy nation, a people belonging to God. (1 PETER 2:9)

FAMILY MATCHUP: HUSBAND AND WIFE—
From this list of men, match each one with the name of his wife in the numbered list below.

HUSBANDS: Abraham Adam Boaz Isaac Jacob Joseph of Nazareth Xerxes Zechariah

1. Elizabeth (**LUKE 1:5**)
2. Esther (**ESTHER 2:8-18**)
3. Eve (**GENESIS 3:20**)
4. Mary (**LUKE 1:26-27**)
5. Rachel (**GENESIS 29**)
6. Rebekah (**GENESIS 24**)
7. Ruth (**RUTH 3—4**)
8. Sarah, or Sarai (**GENESIS 11:29**)

FAMILY MATCHUP: MOTHER AND SON—
From this list of women, match each one with the name of her son in the numbered list below.

MOTHERS: Elizabeth Eve Hannah Mary Rachel Sarah

9. Cain, Abel, and Seth (Genesis 4)
10. Isaac (Genesis 21:1-7)
11. Jacob and Esau (Genesis 25:20-26)
12. John the Baptist (Luke 1)
13. Samuel (1 Samuel 1)
14. Jesus (Matthew 1:16)

FAMILY MATCHUP: FATHER AND SON—
From this list of men, match each one with the name of his son in the numbered list below.

FATHERS: Abraham Adam Isaac Jacob Jesse Noah Saul Zebedee Zechariah

15. Asher, Benjamin, Dan, Gad, Issachar, Joseph, Judah, Levi, Naphtali, Reuben, Simeon, Zebulun (Genesis 35:23–26)
16. Cain, Abel, and Seth (Genesis 4)
17. David (Ruth 4:17)
18. Isaac and Ishmael (Genesis 16, 21:1-5)
19. Jacob and Esau (Genesis 25:20-26)
20. James and John (Mark 1:19-20)
21. John the Baptist (Luke 1)
22. Jonathan (1 Samuel 14)
23. Shem, Ham, and Japheth (Genesis 6:10)

Don't know an ANSWER? Look first in the Bible, then in the back of this book...

The Promised Land

Then the Lord said, "This is the land I promised on oath to Abraham, Isaac and Jacob." (DEUTERONOMY 34:4)

RHYME TIME—

1. Who did God say this to: "Leave this place, you and the people you brought up out of Egypt, and go up to the land I promised on oath to Abraham, Isaac and Jacob"? *(Clue: the answer rhymes with "noses"*—EXODUS 33:1)

2. Supply the missing word: "Go up to the land flowing with milk and _________." *(The answer rhymes with "sunny"* — EXODUS 33:3)

3. Supply the missing word: "The Lord your God has _________ you out of all the peoples on the face of the earth to be his people, his treasured possession." *(The answer rhymes with "frozen"* —DEUTERONOMY 7:6)

WHICH WAY?—

If you were starting a trip from Jerusalem back in Bible times, which direction would you go to get to these places? Match each place name to an arrow on the map.

PLACES: *Negev Desert* *Egypt* *Babylon* *Nazareth* *Rome* *Sodom and Gomorrah*

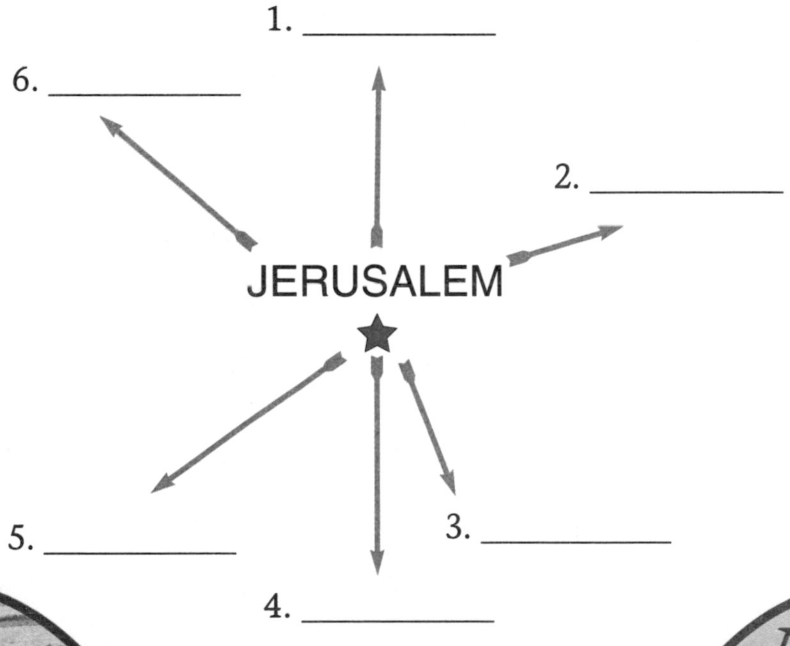

1. ___________

6. ___________

2. ___________

JERUSALEM

5. ___________

3. ___________

4. ___________

N

*Ask and it will be given to you; seek and you will find; knock and the door will be opened to you. (**Jesus,** in MATTHEW 7:7)*

FAMOUS PRAYERS IN THE BIBLE—Tell who prayed each one of these prayers:

1. "Father, the time has come. Glorify your Son, that your Son may glorify you" (JOHN 17:1).
2. "O my God, I am too ashamed and disgraced to lift up my face to you, my God, because our sins are higher than our heads and our guilt has reached to the heavens" (EZRA 9:5–6).
3. "Strike these people with blindness" (2 KINGS 6:18).
4. "O Lord, open his eyes so he may see" (2 KINGS 6:17).

5. "O Lord, God of Abraham, Isaac and Israel, let it be known today that you are God in Israel and that I am your servant and have done all these things at your command. Answer me, O Lord, answer me, so these people will know that you, O Lord, are God, and that you are turning their hearts back again" (1 Kings 18:36-37).

6. "I have had enough, Lord. Take my life; I am no better than my ancestors" (1 Kings 19:3-4).

7. "Who am I, O Sovereign Lord, and what is my family, that you have brought me this far?... How great you are, O Sovereign Lord! There is no one like you, and there is no God but you, as we have heard with our own ears.... And now, Lord God, keep forever the promise you have made concerning your servant and his house. Do as you promised, so that your name will be great forever" (2 Samuel 7:18-26).

8. "O Lord, God of my master Abraham, give me success today, and show kindness to my master Abraham. See, I am standing beside this spring, and the daughters of the townspeople are coming out to draw water. May it be that when I say to a girl, "Please let down your jar that I may have a drink," and she says, 'Drink, and I'll water your camels too' — let her be the one you have chosen for your servant Isaac" (Genesis 24:12-14).

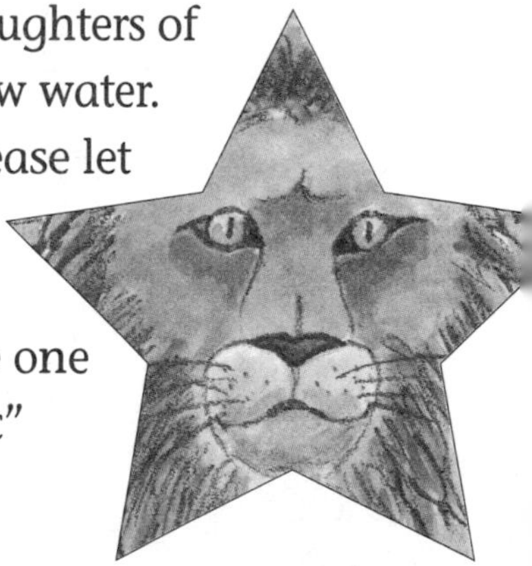

Don't know an ANSWER? Look first in the Bible, then in the back of this book...

The Way of Wisdom

Honey from the comb is sweet to your taste.
Know also that wisdom is sweet to your soul. (PROVERBS 24:13-14)

ABC's—Words that start with each letter of the alphabet will complete these verses from **PROVERBS**, the wisdom book. Use the clue that follows each letter to find the missing word.

A— (CLUE:) *Frightened, scared;* (VERSE:) "Being a_________ of people can get you into trouble. But if you trust the Lord, you will be safe" **(29:25)**.

B— *The son of your mother and father;* "A b_________ is always there to help you" **(17:17)**.

C— *Quiet and peaceful;* "A person who quickly loses his temper does foolish things. But a person with understanding remains c________" **(14:17)**.

D— *Tears up, breaks apart;* "A person who doesn't work hard is just like a person who d__________ things" **(18:9)**.

E— *Not hard;* "Understanding wisdom is as e_______ as getting water from a flowing stream" **(18:4)**.

F— *Unwise, and not caring about pleasing God;* "A f__________ son makes his father sad. And he causes his mother great sorrow" **(17:25)**.

G— *Something you make or buy to present to someone else;* "Taking a g_______ to an important person will help get you in to see him" **(18:16)**.

H— *To cover up, so no one can see;* "If you h_________ your sins, you will not succeed. If you confess and reject them, you will receive mercy" **(28:13)**.

I— *Not guilty;* "No one can say, 'I am i____________. I have never done anything wrong'" **(20:9)**.

J— *Happiness, gladness;* "Strangers cannot share your j_____" **(14:10)**.

CONTINUED ON NEXT PAGE

K— *Causing death;* "Some people think they are doing what's right. But what they are doing will really k______ them" (14:12).

L— *To find out something; to discover it, and to keep it in your mind;* "Teach a wise man, and he will become even wiser. Teach a good man, and he will l______ even more" (9:9).

M—*What you use to buy and spend;* "M_________ that comes easily disappears quickly. But m_________ that is gathered little by little will slowly grow" (13:11).

N—*A country; people living together under the same government;* "Without leadership a n_______ will be defeated. But when many people give advice, it will be safe" (11:14).

O—*People besides yourself;* "Foolish people don't care if they sin. But honest people work at being right with o________" (14:9).

P— *Spoken highly of, complimented;* "A woman who respects the Lord should be p________" (31:30).

Q—*Something you ask, and want answers for;* "The first person to tell his side of a story seems right. But that may change when somebody comes and asks him q__________" (18:17).

R— *Having lots of money;* "A selfish person is in a hurry to get r_______. He does not realize his selfishness will make him poor" (28:22).

S— *Not happy or joyful;* "When someone is laughing, he may be s______ inside" **(14:13).**

T— *What a person does with his mind;* "A foolish person does not want to understand anything. He only enjoys telling others what he t________" **(18:2).**

U— *Not friendly;* "An u___________ person cares only about himself. He makes fun of all wisdom" **(18:1).**

V— *Goes away, disappears;* "Wealth that comes from telling lies v____________ like a mist and leads to death" **(21:6).**

W—*Something spoken;* "Every w_______ of God can be trusted. He protects those who come to him for safety" **(30:5).**

X— *Very much so;* "Four things on earth are small, yet they are ex____________ wise…" **(30:24).**

Y— *Not old;* "These wise words…teach wisdom and self-control…. They give knowledge and good sense to the y________" **(1:1–4).**

Z— *The focus of your eyes, the direction you are looking;* "Let your eyes look straight ahead, fix your ____ze directly before you" **(4:25).**

Don't know an ANSWER? Look first in the Bible, then in the back of this book…

"The Holy Spirit...will teach you all things and will remind you of everything I have said to you." (**Jesus,** *in* JOHN *14:26)*

UNLOCK THE TREASURE BOX:

What's the KEY WORD *(it goes where you see the ***)* in this passage?

____

* * *

(It begins with the letter "O")

"There is *** body and *** Spirit—just as you were called to *** hope when you were called —*** Lord, *** faith, *** baptism; *** God and Father of all, who is over all and through all and in all."

— EPHESIANS **4:4-7**

The Way of Love

Love never fails. (1 Corinthians 13:8)

SWORD-SHARPENERS—"The sword of the Spirit...is the word of God" (Ephesians 6:17). For each verse below, fill in the right word at the beginning — at the "tip of the sword." (When you read down, the first letters of these words will spell the word HEART.)

"H_______ me, O Lord, and I will be healed" (Jeremiah 17:14).

"E_______ of you should look not only to your own interests, but also to the interests of others" (Philippians 2:4).

"A_______ the believers were one in heart and mind" (Acts 4:32).

"R_______ me and deliver me in your righteousness" (Psalm 71:2).

"T_______ my yoke upon you and learn from me, for I am gentle and humble in heart" (Matthew 11:29).

Don't know an ANSWER? Look first in the Bible, then in the back of this book...

What Happened When?

And God said, "Let there be lights in the expanse of the sky to separate the day from the night, and let them serve as signs to mark seasons and days and years." (Genesis 1:14)

TIME LINE: Match the following events with the approximate date shown beside the time line on the next page.

1. Because she is already ninety years old, Sarah laughs when she hears the Lord say she will have a son. (**Genesis 18:10-15**)
2. Because he will not give praise to God, King Herod is eaten by worms and dies. (**Acts 12:19-23**)
3. Moses gives Pharaoh a message from God: "Let My people go!" (**Exodus 10:3**)

4. Saul and his son Jonathan die in the same battle. (1 SAMUEL 31)

5. At different times on the same day, the prophets Elijah and Elisha cause the waters of the Jordan River to split apart. (2 KINGS 2)

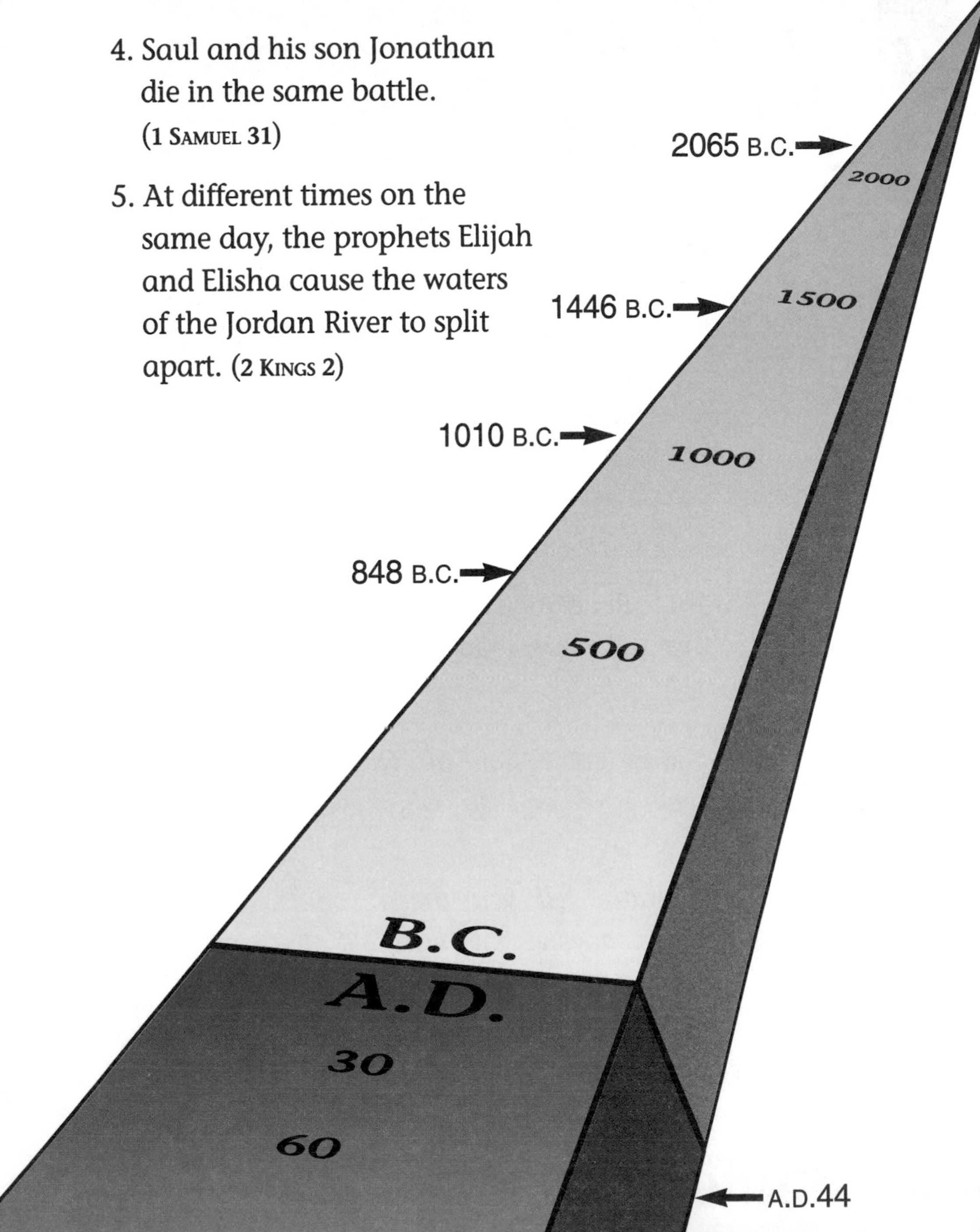

Jesus lives forever.... He is always able to save those who come to God through him. (HEBREWS *7:24-25*)

SCRIPTURE SCRAMBLE: Rearrange the words in each numbered sentence below so that the verses read correctly.

1. *Man came Son of The*
lost. seek save and to what was to

LUKE 19:10

2. *truth, tell you the I*
keeps anyone my word, if
death. he never see will

JOHN 8:51

3. *blood covenant, is of This the my*
poured which is out many for
sins. the forgiveness for of

MATTHEW 26:28

4. *life. am resurrection and I the the*
live, believes who in me will He
dies; though he even
lives and whoever and in me believes
die. will never

JOHN 11:25-26

5. *loves life lose will man who his it, The*
man hates who the life his while
this world in
life. keep eternal will it for

JOHN 12:25

6. *this: work God The is of*
believe one to in he sent. has the

JOHN 6:29

7. *bread the am life. I of*
hungry, He who to me will never go comes
believes and he in me who
thirsty. will be never

JOHN 6:35

Don't know an ANSWER? Look first in the Bible, then in the back of this book…

Praise be to the Lord my Rock, who trains my hands for war, my fingers for battle. (*Psalm 144:1*)

WORDS OF KINGS AND COMMANDERS: Which ruler or military leader in the Bible made each of these statements?

1. "Put Uriah in the front line where the fighting is fiercest. Then withdraw from him so he will be struck down and die" (2 Samuel 11:15).
2. "Bring me a sword. Cut the living child in two and give half to one and half to the other" (1 Kings 3:24-25).
3. "What have we done? We have let the Israelites go and have lost their services!" (Exodus 14:5).

4. "The Lord has driven out before you great and powerful nations; to this day no one has been able to withstand you. One of you routs a thousand, because the Lord your God fights for you, just as he promised. So be very careful to love the Lord your God" (JOSHUA 23:9-11).

5. "Intercede with the Lord your God and pray for me that my hand may be restored" (1 KINGS 13:6).

6. "I thought that he would surely come out to me and stand and call on the name of the Lord his God, wave his hand over the spot and cure me of my leprosy. Are not Abana and Pharpar, the rivers of Damascus, better than any of the waters of Israel? Couldn't I wash in them and be cleansed?" (2 KINGS 5:11-12).

7. "You are more righteous than I. You have treated me well, but I have treated you badly. You have just now told me of the good you did to me; the Lord delivered me into your hands, but you did not kill me" (1 SAMUEL 24:17-18).

8. "Here I am, living in a palace of cedar, while the ark of God remains in a tent" (2 SAMUEL 7:2).

9. "Go throughout the tribes of Israel from Dan to Beersheba and enroll the fighting men, so that I may know how many there are" (2 SAMUEL 24:2).

Coming Kingdom

I will not drink of this fruit of the vine again until that day when I drink it new with you in my Father's kingdom. (***Jesus,*** *in* MATTHEW *26:29)*

SCRIPTURE SCRAMBLE: Rearrange the words in each numbered sentence below so that these "kingdom sayings" of Jesus read correctly.

1. *darkened, The be will sun*
   moon and not the will its give light;
   fall stars will the from the sky,
   shaken. and the bodies be heavenly will

   MATTHEW **24:29**

2. *keep Therefore watch,*
   you know because do what not on day
   your come. Lord will

   MATTHEW **24:42**

I remind you to fan into flame the gift of God which is in you.
(2 Timothy 1:6)

SWORD-SHARPENERS—"The sword of the Spirit…is the word of God" (Ephesians 6:17). For each verse below, fill in the right word at the beginning — at the "tip of the sword." (When you read down, the first letters of these words will spell the word FLAME.)

"F_______ the good fight of the faith" (1 Timothy 6:12).

"L_______ me, O Lord, in your righteousness" (Psalm 5:8).

"A_______ for perfection, listen to my appeal, be of one mind, live in peace" (2 Corinthians 13:11).

"M_______ every effort to live in peace with all men" (Hebrews 12:14).

"E_______ who has this hope in him purifies himself, just as he is pure" (1 John 3:3).

Don't know an ANSWER? Look first in the Bible, then in the back of this book…

The Great Battle

Our fight is not against people on earth.... We are fighting against the spiritual powers of evil in the heavenly world. (Ephesians 6:12)

THE ENEMY—

1. Jesus called him "a liar and the father of lies," and "a murderer from the beginning" (John 8:44). In Revelation 9:11, he is called "the angel of the Abyss"; he also has the names "Abaddon" (in Hebrew) and "Apollyon" (in Greek), which both mean *Destroyer.* In Genesis 3 he takes the form of a serpent. He also has the names "Belial" (2 Corinthians 6:15), "Beelzebub" (Matthew 10:25), and the "evil one" (1 John 3:12). Who is this?

2. What will happen to him at the end of time? (Revelation 20:10)

“ ”

WHO SAID THIS?

Tell who made each of these statements in the Scriptures:

1. “Every boy that is born you must throw into the Nile, but let every girl live” (Exodus 1:22).
2. “I baptize with water, but among you stands one you do not know. He is the one who comes after me, the thongs of whose sandals I am not worthy to untie” (John 1:26-27).
3. “It is not good for man to be alone” (Genesis 2:18).
4. “Silver or gold I do not have, but what I have I give to you. In the name of Jesus Christ of Nazareth, walk” (Acts 3:6).
5. “Look, Lord! Here and now I give half of my possessions to the poor, and if I have cheated anybody out of anything, I will pay back four times the amount” (Luke 19:8).
6. “Come, make us gods who will go before us. As for this fellow Moses who brought us up out of Egypt, we don’t know what has happened to him” (Exodus 32:1).
7. “Then they gave me the gold, and I threw it into the fire, and out came this calf!” (Exodus 32:24).
8. “Oh, that someone would get me a drink of water from the well near the gate of Bethlehem!” (2 Samuel 23:15).

Treasure Chest

Store up for yourselves treasures in heaven, where moth and rust do not destroy, and where thieves do not break in and steal.
*(**Jesus,** in MATTHEW 6:20)*

SWORD-SHARPENERS—"The sword of the Spirit…is the word of God" (**EPHESIANS 6:17**). For each verse below, fill in the right word at the beginning — at the "tip of the sword." (When you read down, the first letters of these words will spell the word GOLD.)

"G_______, and it will be given to you" (**LUKE 6:38**).

"O_______ my eyes that I may see wonderful things in your law" (**PSALM 119:18**).

"L_______ us then approach the throne of grace with confidence, so that we may receive mercy and find grace to help us in our time of need" (**HEBREWS 4:16**).

"D_______ yourself in the Lord and he will give you the desires of your heart" (**PSALM 37:4**).

KINGDOM TREASURE:

1. In Matthew 13:45-46, Jesus said that the kingdom of God is like a man who did something in order to buy a very expensive pearl. What did the man do?

2. In Matthew 13:44, Jesus said the kingdom of God is like a man who did something in order to buy a field that had treasure buried in it. What did this man do?

♥ How much do you want to be a part of God's kingdom? What are you willing to give up in order to be a part of His kingdom?

3

The Sovereign Lord will wipe away the tears from all faces.
(Isaiah 25:8)

READ THESE CLUES CAREFULLY:

These two famous places in Israel are only five miles apart.
The names of both places end with the letters EM.
Place Number 1 is most famous because of who was born there;
Place Number 2 is famous because of who died there…and it's the same person in both places. (**Matthew 2:1, 16:21**)

1. What's the name of Place Number 1?
2. What's the name of Place Number 2?
3. Name the person who was born in Place Number 1 and died in Place Number 2.

4. What is the name of the place where the people of Israel lived while they were in Egypt? (GENESIS 45:10, EXODUS 8:22)

5. What was the name of the city where the people set up the Tent of Meeting after Joshua led them to victory in taking over Canaan? It's also the place where Eli and Samuel ministered to the Lord. (JOSHUA 18:1-10; 1 SAMUEL 1:24-28)

6. What is another name for Jerusalem—one of David's favorite names for that city? *(Clue: It has four letters, and it begins with "Z"—* 2 SAMUEL 5:7; PSALM 9:11, 14:7, 20:2, 51:18, 53:6, 65:1, 69:35, 110:2, 133:3)

▼▼▼

The kingdom of Israel, which became strong under David and his son Solomon, became divided into two kingdoms after Solomon's son Rehoboam became king. Of the twelve tribes of Israel, ten became part of the northern kingdom (with Samaria as the capital), and two tribes stayed loyal to David's descendants, and kept their capital in Jerusalem.

7. By what name was the southern kingdom of two tribes known by? (1 KINGS 14:21, 15:1, 15:9)

8. By what name was the northern kingdom of ten tribes known by? (1 KINGS 16:5, 16:14, 16:20)

Don't know an ANSWER? Look first in the Bible, then in the back of this book...

Jesus Our Friend

I have called you friends, for everything that I learned from my Father I have made known to you. (***Jesus***, *in* JOHN *15:15*)

SWORD-SHARPENERS—"The sword of the Spirit…is the word of God" (**EPHESIANS 6:17**). Fill in the right word at the tip of each "sword" below. (The first letters of the words will spell the word JESUS .)

"J_______ as Moses lifted up the snake in the desert, so the Son of Man must be lifted up, that everyone who believes in him may have eternal life" (**JOHN 3:14**).

"E_______ the wind and the waves obey him" (**MARK 4:41**).

"S_______ to it, then, that the light within you is not darkness" (**LUKE 11:35**).

"U_______ now you have not asked for anything in my name. Ask and you will receive, and your joy will be complete" (**JOHN 16:24**).

"S_______ is good, but if it loses its saltiness, how can you make it salty again? Have salt in yourselves, and be at peace with each other" (**MARK 9:50**).

SCRIPTURE SCRAMBLE: JESUS AND THE HOLY SPIRIT—
Rearrange the words in each numbered sentence to repeat correctly these words Jesus spoke about the Holy Spirit:

1. *truth comes, When the Spirit of guide he will you all truth. into*

JOHN 16:13

2. *from mine what is will take Spirit The and to you. it make known*

JOHN 16:15

3. *I the Father, will ask will he you give Counselor another and you with forever— to be the of truth. Spirit*

JOHN 14:16-17

4. *Counselor, the Holy Spirit, The whom will send the Father my name, in all things you will teach everything will remind you of and have you. said to I*

JOHN 14:26

5. *then, though you you are evil, If gifts good give to your children, how to know how more will your Father much in heaven Spirit Holy give the him! ask who those to*

LUKE 11:13

Don't know an ANSWER? Look first in the Bible, then in the back of this book…

They were brave warriors, ready for battle... Their faces were the faces of lions...they were as swift as gazelles in the mountains. (1 Chronicles 12:8)

FIRE!

1. Who went up to heaven in a chariot of fire? (2 Kings 2)
2. Who tied burning torches to the tails of 300 foxes, and sent them running through the grainfields of the Philistines? (Judges 15)
3. Who saw God send down fire and burn up the altar he had built on Mount Carmel? (1 Kings 18)
4. Who got bit by a snake while he was putting wood on a fire? (Acts 28:1-6)
5. Who heard God's voice speaking from a burning bush? (Exodus 3)

6. Who stayed alive after being thrown into a furnace of fire? (DANIEL 3)
7. This follower of Jesus was warming himself by a fire in an outdoor courtyard while Jesus was inside being spoken against by the Jewish leaders. Who was he? (MARK 14:53–65)
8. Who told his three hundred men to carry jars with torches inside them? (JUDGES 7:15-21)
9. Whose words of prophecy, written on a scroll, were thrown into a fire by an evil king? (JEREMIAH 36)
10. Who returned with his men to the town of Ziklag, and found that their wives and all their children had been taken away, and the city burned down by the Amalekites? (1 SAMUEL 30:1–2)
11. Who built an altar and offered burnt sacrifices on it to God after being saved from a flood? (GENESIS 8:20)
12. This man went into the Temple in Jerusalem to burn incense to the Lord. While he was there, God told him that his wife was going to have a son. Who was this man? (LUKE 1:8-17)

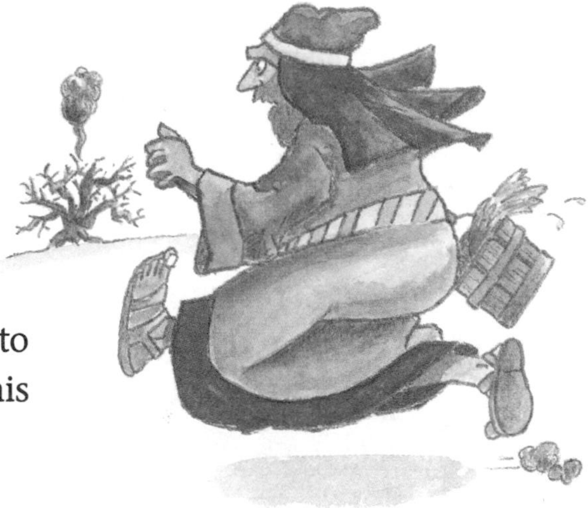

SHOUTS IN THE BIBLE

WHO SHOUTED THIS?—Tell who spoke each one of these shouts in the Bible:

1. *On the hill called Golgotha:* "My God, my God, why have you forsaken me?" (MATTHEW 27:46).
2. *In the countryside of Judah:* "Why do you come out and line up for battle? Am I not a Philistine, and are you not the servants of Saul?" (1 SAMUEL 17:8).
3. *In a jail in Philippi:* "Don't harm yourself! We are all here!" (ACTS 16:28).
4. *In Babylon:* "Shadrach, Meshach and Abednego, servants of the Most High God, come out! Come here!" (DANIEL 3:26).
5. *On Mount Carmel:* "O Baal, answer us!" (1 KINGS 18:26).
6. *In the temple of the Philistine god Dagon:* "Bring out Samson to entertain us" (JUDGES 16:23-25).
7. *In Isaac's tent:* "Bless me—me too, my father!" (GENESIS 27:34).
8. *On the road into Jerusalem:* "Hosanna to the Son of David!" (MATTHEW 21:9).
9. *Outside the governor's palace in Jerusalem:* "Crucify! Crucify!" (JOHN 19:6).
10. *At a tomb near Bethany:* "Lazarus, come out!" (JOHN 11:43).

The Lord is faithful to all his promises. (PSALM 145:13)

PROMISE POWER—Match the right ending *(from the list below)* to each of these powerful promises in God's Word.

1. If we confess our sins, he is faithful and just…
2. I tell you the truth, he who believes…
3. Whoever has my commands and obeys them, he is the one who loves me. He who loves me will be loved by my Father,…

(A)• *and will forgive us our sins and purify us from all unrighteousness* (1 JOHN 1:9).

(B)• *has everlasting life* (Jesus, in JOHN 6:47).

(C)• *and I too will love him and show myself to him* (Jesus, in JOHN 14:21).

Don't know an ANSWER? Look first in the Bible, then in the back of this book…

I will remember the deeds of the Lord; yes, I will remember your miracles of long ago. (PSALM 77:11)

WHICH CAME FIRST? In the week of Creation (GENESIS 1)—when God created everything—which did He make first?

1. the sun <u>or</u> sunflowers?
2. light <u>or</u> land?
3. starfish <u>or</u> stars?
4. oceans <u>or</u> ostriches?
5. the sky <u>or</u> skunks?
6. ants <u>or</u> Adam?
7. raccoons <u>or</u> roses?
8. sheep <u>or</u> sharks?

IT HAPPENED AGAIN!

In Matthew 14, Jesus gave 5,000 hungry men (plus many women and children) all the fish and bread they could eat, though He started with only five loaves and two fish.

In the next chapter of Matthew's gospel (15:32-39), we read about a similar miracle.

9. *This second time,* how many loaves of bread did Jesus start with?

10. *This second time,* how many fish did He start with?

11. *This second time,* how many people did He feed?

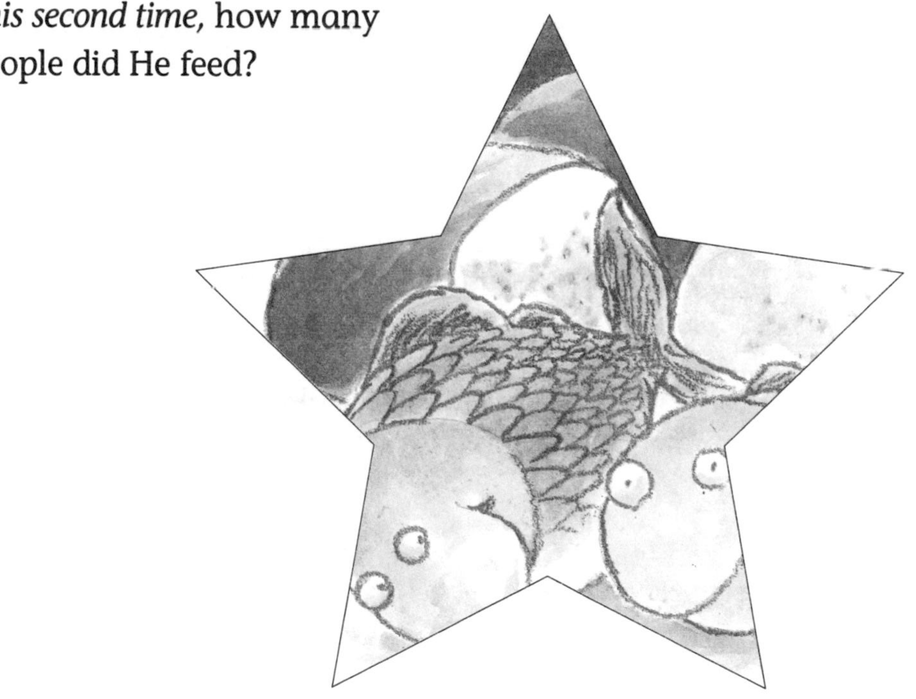

Don't know an ANSWER? Look first in the Bible, then in the back of this book...

Knowing God

We will not fear even if the oceans roar and foam, or if the mountains shake at the raging sea.... God says, "Be quiet and know that I am God." (PSALM 46:3-10)

WHERE TO GO TO LEARN ABOUT GOD:

1. Supply the two missing words in this statement Jesus made to His disciples: "If you really knew me, you would know ____ ____________ as well" (JOHN 14:7).
2. Jesus also made this statement (supply the missing word): "Anyone who has seen me has seen the ____________" (JOHN 14:9).
3. According to 2 Timothy 3:16, who "inspired" or "breathed out" the words of Scripture?

WONDER WORDS—Can you supply the missing word in each of these verses?

4. Without ______ it is impossible to please God. (HEBREWS 11:6; *the word means "believing," or "trusting."*)

5. *(This word is used three times at the beginning of this verse:)* ______, ______, ______ is the Lord Almighty; the whole earth is full of his glory. (ISAIAH 6:3; *the word means that God is set apart, and different, and that He can't even be touched by any evil.)*

6. God is ________, and his worshipers must worship in ________ *(same word)* and in truth, for they are the kind of worshipers the Father seeks. (JOHN 4:24; *the word tells us that God isn't kept inside a physical body like we are here on earth.)*

7. For it is by _________ you have been saved, through faith—and this not from yourselves, it is the gift of God. (EPHESIANS 2:8; *this word means the rich gifts God gives us without our earning or deserving them.)*

8. The Lord is ______ to all his promises. (PSALM 145:13; *it means that God always keeps His promises.)*

9. For the Lord is ________, he loves justice; upright men will see his face. (PSALM 11:7; *the word means that God always does what is right.)*

♥ What to you are the most important things to learn about God?

Don't know an ANSWER? Look first in the Bible, then in the back of this book...

Born Again

I tell you the truth, no one can see the kingdom of God unless he is born again. (***Jesus****, in* J*OHN* *3:3*)

TRIPLE SEARCH:

How many words can you find that are included in ALL THREE of these verses?

The goal of this command is love, which comes from a pure heart and a good conscience and a sincere faith. (1 TIMOTHY 1:5)

Pursue righteousness, faith, love and peace, along with those who call on the Lord out of a pure heart. (2 TIMOTHY 2:22)

Blessed are the pure in heart, for they will see God. (MATTHEW 5:8)

WHAT'S THAT I HEAR?

1. We're with the prophet Ezekiel in a valley filled with bones that are very dry. God has brought Ezekiel here, and has commanded him to tell His message to the bones. As Ezekiel calls out that message, there's a rattling sound. What is this rattling noise? (Ezekiel 37:1–14)

2. We're with the first followers of Jesus, who are all together in a house on the day of Pentecost, not long after Jesus went back into heaven. Suddenly there's a sound like a wild rushing wind, and then there's the sound of all the Christians speaking in different languages. Who is causing this? (Acts 2:1-11)

3. We're with Abraham on Mount Moriah. God has commanded him to come here and to offer his son Isaac as a sacrifice. Abraham has obeyed. He brought Isaac here, built an altar, and put wood on the altar for the fire. Then he tied up Isaac and laid him on the wood. Now Abraham is holding a knife, and his hand is raised up to kill his son, whom he loves so much. But suddenly there's a voice from heaven. What does the voice say? (Genesis 22:1-14)

Be Strong in the Lord

The name of the Lord is a strong tower; the righteous run to it and are safe. (PROVERBS 18:10)

WORDS OF DUTY —Tell who made each of these statements in the Scriptures:

1. "So you also, when you have done everything you were told to do, should say, 'We are unworthy servants; we have only done our duty'" (LUKE 17:10).
2. "I am about to go the way of all the earth. So be strong, show yourself a man, and observe what the Lord your God requires" (1 KINGS 2:2-3).
3. "We must go through many hardships to enter the kingdom of God" (ACTS 14:22).

★ GOLD STAR SPECIAL ★

STRONG FINISHES — Name the New Testament book that ends with each of these verses:

1. Jesus did many other things as well. If every one of them were written down, I suppose that even the whole world would not have room for the books that would be written.
2. Greet one another with a kiss of love. Peace to all of you who are in Christ.
3. For two whole years Paul stayed there in his own rented house and welcomed all who came to see him. Boldly and without hindrance he preached the kingdom of God and taught about the Lord Jesus Christ.
4. Then Jesus came to them and said, "All authority in heaven and on earth has been given to me. Therefore go and make disciples of all nations, baptizing them in the name of the Father and of the Son and of the Holy Spirit, and teaching them to obey everything I have commanded you. And surely I am with you always, to the very end of the age."
5. Finally, let no one cause me trouble, for I bear on my body the marks of Jesus. The grace of our Lord Jesus Christ be with your spirit, brothers. Amen.
6. Dear children, keep yourselves from idols.

Bible Numbers

How precious to me are your thoughts, O God!
How vast is the sum of them! Were I to count them,
they would outnumber the grains of sand. (PSALM 139:17-18)

BIG NUMBERS—

1. What is the biggest number in the Bible? (**REVELATION 9:16**)
2. Who was the oldest man in the Bible? (**GENESIS 5:27**)
3. How long did he live? (**GENESIS 5:27**)
4. Who was the second oldest man in the Bible? (**GENESIS 5:20**)
5. How long did he live? (**GENESIS 5:20**)
6. Who was the third oldest man in the Bible? (**GENESIS 9:29**)
7. How long did he live? (**GENESIS 9:29**)

When Tough Times Come

★★★

Some were laughed at and beaten. Others were tied and put into prison. They were killed with stones and they were cut in half. (HEBREWS 11:36-37)

UNLOCK THE TREASURE BOX:

What's the KEY WORD *(it goes where you see the* ***) in this passage?

______

* * *

(It begins with the letter "D")

"My son, do not make light of the Lord's ***, and do not lose heart when he rebukes you, because the Lord ***s those he loves.... Endure hardship as ***; God is treating you as sons. For what son is not ***d by his father? God ***s us for our good, that we may share in his holiness." — **HEBREWS 12:5-10**

Children are a gift from the Lord. (Psalm 127:3)

FAMILY MATCHUP: BROTHER AND BROTHER—
From this list of men, match each one with the name of his brother in the numbered list below. And imagine what it was like when they were children growing up together.

Abel Esau James Moses Peter

1. Aaron (**Exodus 4:14**)
2. Andrew (**Matthew 4:18**)
3. Cain and Seth (**Genesis 4**)
4. Jacob (**Genesis 25:20-26**)
5. John (**Matthew 4:21**)

FAMILY MATCHUP: SISTER AND SISTER—
From this list of women, match each one with the name of her sister in the numbered list below. And imagine what it was like when they were children growing up together.

Mary Merab Rachel

6. Leah (Genesis 29:16)
7. Martha (Luke 10:38-42)
8. Michal (1 Samuel 18:17-20)

FAMILY MATCHUP: BROTHER AND SISTER—
From this list of men, match each one with the name of his sister in the numbered list below. And imagine what it was like when they were children growing up together.

Absalom Laban Lazarus Simeon and Levi

9. Dinah (Genesis 34)
10. Mary and Martha (John 11:1-3)
11. Rebekah (Genesis 24:29)
12. Tamar (2 Samuel 13:1)

Don't know an ANSWER? Look first in the Bible, then in the back of this book...

Many women do noble things.... A woman who respects the Lord should be praised. (PROVERBS 31:29-30)

1. She was the daughter of Israel's first king, and the wife of Israel's second king. Who was she? (1 SAMUEL 18:27)
2. She had to try four times before she finally got Samson to tell her the secret of his strength. Who was she? (JUDGES 16)
3. When she saw her husband jumping and dancing before the Lord, "she despised him in her heart." Who was she? (2 SAMUEL 6:16)
4. She wandered with her son in the desert. When she had no more water, she sat down and began to cry. Then an angel came, and her eyes were opened and she saw a well of water. Who was she? (GENESIS 21:14-21)

WORDS FROM WOMEN—Name the woman who spoke each of these things in the Bible:

5. "They have no more wine" (John 2:3).
6. "Not so, my lord. I am a woman who is deeply troubled. I have not been drinking wine or beer; I was pouring out my soul to the Lord" (1 Samuel 1:15).
7. "Return home, my daughters. Why would you come with me? Am I going to have any more sons, who could become your husbands?" (Ruth 1:11-13).
8. "Very well, I will go with you. But because of the way you are going about this, the honor will not be yours, for the Lord will hand Sisera over to a woman" (Judges 4:9).
9. "When we heard of it, our hearts melted and everyone's courage failed because of you, for the Lord your God is God in heaven above and on the earth below. Now then, please swear to me by the Lord that you will show kindness to my family, because I have shown kindness to you. Give me a sure sign that you will spare the lives of my father and mother, my brothers and sisters, and all who belong to them, and that you will save us from death" (Joshua 2:11-13).
10. "Sing to the Lord, for he is highly exalted. The horse and its rider he has hurled into the sea" (Exodus 15:21).

You should recognize the value of men like these.
(1 Corinthians 16:18)

1. Jesus took three of His disciples high on a mountain. There He was changed; His face became as bright as the sun, and His clothes as white as light. Then two Old Testament men appeared, and they talked with Jesus. Who were these two men from the past? (Matthew 17:1–3)

SCRIPTURE SCRAMBLE: Arrange in the right order these words from Psalm 112:1, Proverbs 3:13, and Psalm 40:4—

2. *man the Lord. who is fears Blessed the*
3. *man Blessed the wisdom. who finds is*
4. *man is the who Blessed makes trust. Lord his the*

LETTER SCRAMBLE: Hidden among the following strange words are some actual names of men in the Bible—written *backwards.* Find them all, using the clues below.

BELOKAR	DELOHOR	DIVAD	ENOSEG
HAON	JULIMAK	LEHAZIM	LEUMAS
LEINAD	MAHARBA	NOSMAS	OKABOL
RETEP	SAMAKA	TELEDOB	SESOM

5. God took this man outside one night and asked him to try counting the stars. (Genesis 15:1–6, 17:4)
6. God gave this man great strength, though for much of his life he wasted it. (Judges 13—16)
7. This shepherd boy became Israel's king; he was called "a man after God's heart." (1 Samuel 16, 13:14; Acts 13:22)
8. This great man of prayer did what he knew God wanted him to do—even when it meant being thrown to the lions. (Daniel 6)
9. God used this prophet and judge to anoint Israel's first two kings. (1 Samuel 9—10, 16)
10. Jesus gave him his name; it means "Rock." (Mark 3:16, John 1:42)
11. God gave him the promise that the earth would never again be flooded. (Genesis 9:8–17)
12. He met the living God in a burning bush. (Exodus 3)

Don't know an ANSWER? Look first in the Bible, then in the back of this book…

Our Home in Heaven

Our homeland is in heaven, and we are waiting for our Savior, the Lord Jesus Christ, to come from heaven. (PHILIPPIANS 3:20)

PLANT THE SEEDS—"The seed is the word of God," Jesus said (LUKE 8:11). In each planter-pot, select the right "seed-word"—the word that makes the verse complete, ready to grow in your heart.

SEED-WORDS to choose from:

time glory treasures guiding trouble greatness

1. ______________
You will keep on g________ me all my life with your wisdom and counsel, and afterwards receive me into the glories of heaven!
(PSALM 73:24)

2. ______________
Since we are his children, we will share his t________ —for all God gives to his Son Jesus is now ours too. But if we are to share his glory, we must also share his suffering.
(ROMANS 8:17)

“ ”

THE VOICE OF GOD

Each of these statements was spoken in the Scriptures by God. For each one, tell who God was speaking to.

1. “I will greatly increase your pains in childbearing; with pain you will give birth to children” (Genesis 3:16).
2. “Leave here, turn eastward and hide in the Kerith Ravine, east of the Jordan. You will drink from the brook, and I have ordered the ravens to feed you there” (1 Kings 17:2-4).
3. “Take courage! As you have testified about me in Jerusalem, so you must also testify in Rome” (Acts 23:11).
4. “The Lord does not look at the things man looks at. Man looks at the outward appearance, but the Lord looks at the heart” (1 Samuel 16:7).
5. “Who gave man his mouth? Who makes him deaf or mute? Who gives him sight or makes him blind? Is it not I, the Lord? Now go; I will help you speak and will teach you what to say” (Exodus 4:11-12).
6. “When a prophet of the Lord is among you, I reveal myself to him in visions. I speak to him in dreams. But this is not true of my servant Moses; he is faithful in all my house. With him I speak face to face, clearly and not in riddles; he sees the form of the Lord. Why then were you not afraid to speak against my servant Moses?” (Numbers 12:6-8).

Book, Chapter & Verse

These words are like nails that have been driven in firmly. They are wise teachings that come from God the Shepherd. (*Ecclesiastes 12:11*)

WHICH BOOK in the Bible…

1. tells about God's creation of the world—**Genesis, Daniel**, or **Isaiah?**
2. tells about Moses and Pharaoh in Egypt—**Amos, Exodus**, or **Romans?**
3. tells about the Ten Commandments—**Philippians, Jeremiah**, or **Exodus?**
4. tells about Gideon—**Deuteronomy, Proverbs**, or **Judges?**
5. tells about Nicodemus—**Nehemiah, John**, or **Revelation?**
6. tells about Paul getting shipwrecked—**1 Thessalonians, Romans**, or **Acts?**
7. tells the most about heaven—**Esther, Revelation**, or **James?**

THREE-SIXTEEN—Each of the passages below is verse 16 of chapter 3 in one of the books of the Bible. Can you tell which book each verse is from? (If you need help, refer to the book names listed on the next page.)

8. For God so loved the world that he gave his one and only Son, that whoever believes in him shall not perish but have eternal life. *(Jesus' words to Nicodemus)*
9. So, because you are lukewarm—neither hot nor cold—I am about to spit you out of my mouth. *(Jesus' words to the church in Laodicea)*
10. All Scripture is God-breathed and is useful for teaching, rebuking, correcting and training in righteousness. *(these words were written by Paul)*
11. Shadrach, Meshach and Abednego replied to the king, "O Nebuchadnezzar, we do not need to defend ourselves before you in this matter." *(and they proved it!)*
12. Don't you know that you yourselves are God's temple and that God's Spirit lives in you? *(Paul's words)*
13. To the woman he said, "I will greatly increase your pains in childbearing; with pain you will give birth to children. Your desire will be for your husband, and he will rule over you." *(God's words to Eve)*
14. Long life is in her right hand; in her left hand are riches and honor. *(Solomon's words about wisdom)*

CONTINUED ON NEXT PAGE

15. By faith in the name of Jesus, this man whom you see and know was made strong. It is Jesus' name and the faith that comes through him that has given this complete healing to him, as you can all see. *(Peter's words to a crowd near the Temple in Jerusalem)*
16. Let the word of Christ dwell in you richly as you teach and admonish one another with all wisdom, and as you sing psalms, hymns and spiritual songs with gratitude in your hearts to God. *(Paul's words)*
17. Go, assemble the elders of Israel and say to them, "The Lord, the God of your fathers—the God of Abraham, Isaac and Jacob—appeared to me and said: I have watched over you and have seen what has been done to you in Egypt." *(God's words to Moses)*

ACTS, COLOSSIANS, 1 CORINTHIANS, DANIEL, EXODUS, GENESIS, JOHN, PROVERBS, REVELATION, 2 TIMOTHY

This is what God said about the angels: "God makes his angels become like winds. He makes his servants become like flames of fire." (HEBREWS 1:7)

ANGELS IN ACTS—Who did an angel speak these words to:

1. "Go south to the road—the desert road—that goes down from Jerusalem to Gaza" (ACTS 8:26).
2. "Your prayers and gifts to the poor have come up as a memorial offering before God" (ACTS 10:4).
3. "Put on your clothes and sandals" (ACTS 12:8).
4. "Do not be afraid. You must stand trial before Caesar; and God has graciously given you the lives of all who sail with you" (ACTS 27:24).
5. "Why do you stand here looking into the sky? This same Jesus, who has been taken from you into heaven, will come back in the same way you have seen him go" (ACTS 1:11).

Don't know an ANSWER? Look first in the Bible, then in the back of this book...

Bible Commands

Loving God means obeying his commands.
And God's commands are not too hard for us. (1 John 5:3)

Moses was up on Mount Sinai (Exodus 32:1-8), receiving the Ten Commandments and other good laws from God. His brother Aaron and the rest of God's people were down below, and they thought it was taking Moses an awfully long time to come back down. They wanted something to worship. So they made something out of gold.

1. What did they make out of gold? (32:4)

2. Where did they get the gold? (32:2–3)

3. What did they say about the thing they had made? (32:4)

God told Moses what the people had done, and He told Moses to go down to them. (Exodus 32:7–10)

4. What did Moses do for the people before he went down to them? (32:11–14)
5. When Moses went down and saw what the people had made and what they were doing, what did he do with the two stone tablets on which God had written the Ten Commandments? (32:15–19)
6. What did Moses do with the thing the people had made out of gold? (*Hint:* He needed fire and water to do it; 32:20.)

God Became a Man

He was equal with God. But he did not think that being equal with God was something to be held on to.... He was born to be a man and became like a servant. (PHILIPPIANS 2:6-7)

WHAT DID JESUS SAY?—Answer "Jesus" for each of these statements in the gospel of Luke which Jesus made; answer "Someone Else" for each one which Jesus did not make:

1. "The Spirit of the Lord is on me, because he has anointed me to preach good news to the poor" (LUKE 4:18).
2. "All things have been committed to me by my Father" (LUKE 10:22).
3. "Go away from me...I am a sinful man" (LUKE 5:8).
4. "This is my body given for you" (LUKE 22:19).
5. "I do not even consider myself worthy to come to you" (LUKE 7:7).

6. In the gospels, and especially in the gospel of Luke, Jesus called Himself by one particular title more often than any other. Tell what it is: The S____ of M____. (LUKE 5:24)

That same title is used for Him in the Old Testament, in a vision which the prophet Daniel had of the coming Messiah (DANIEL 7:13–14). Complete the part of Daniel's prophecy listed here by adding the right words in the right places. Choose them from the list of words below (not all of them will be used).

"In my vision at (7) n______ I looked, and there before me was one like a (8) s____ of (9) m____, coming with the clouds of (10) h________. He approached the Ancient of Days and was led into his presence. He was given authority, (11) g______ and sovereign power; all peoples, (12) n________ and men of every language worshiped him. His dominion is an everlasting (13) d_________ that will not pass away, and his kingdom is one that will never be (14) d_________."

might *nations* *star* *glory* *destroyed*

holy *night* *delivered* *heaven*

man *dominion* *grief* *son*

Jesus Our Leader

*You call me "Teacher" and "Lord." And this is right, because that is what I am. (**Jesus,** in JOHN 13:13)*

WHICH HAPPENED <u>FIRST</u>?

1. Jesus turned water into wine at a wedding in Cana, <u>or</u> Jesus spoke to Zacchaeus in the tree? (**JOHN 2:1–11, LUKE 19:1-10**)
2. Peter said he believed that Jesus is the Christ, the Son of God, <u>or</u> Jesus told the disciples for the first time that He must suffer and die? (**MATTHEW 16:13-28**)
3. Jesus washed the disciples' feet, <u>or</u> Jesus told the disciples that He would be betrayed? (**JOHN 13:1–30**)

SCRIPTURE SCRAMBLE: Rearrange the words in each numbered sentence below so that the verses read correctly.

4. *come If would after me, anyone*
himself must deny he
daily take and up his cross
follow me. and

LUKE 9:23

5. *world. I am the light of the*
follows Whoever me
darkness, never will walk in
light have will the of life. but

JOHN 8:12

6. *follow Whoever me must me; serves*
where and I am,
my also will be. servant

JOHN 12:26

7. *light, I come have into world as a the*
that so no believes in me who one
darkness. should in stay

JOHN 12:46

8. *pass and earth will away, Heaven*
never pass but words will away. my

MATTHEW 24:35

Bold and Brave

The righteous are as bold as a lion. (PROVERBS 28:1)

PLANT THE SEEDS—"The seed is the word of God," Jesus said (LUKE 8:11). In each planter-pot, plant the right "seed-word"—the word that makes the verse complete, ready to grow in your heart.

SEED-WORDS to choose from:

star signal sight stand strong separate

1. ______________

Most people will stop showing their love for each other. But the person who continues to be s_______ until the end will be saved.
(MATTHEW 24:12–13)

2. ______________

Yes, I am sure that nothing can s__________ us from the love God has for us.... from the love of God that is in Christ Jesus our Lord.
(ROMANS 8:38–39)

WHO SAID THIS?

Tell who made each of these statements in Scripture:

1. "Let us make man in our image, in our likeness, and let him rule over the fish of the sea and the birds of the air, over the livestock, over all the earth, and over all the creatures that move along the ground" (Genesis 1:26).
2. "Surely the Lord is in this place, and I was not aware of it.... How awesome is this place! This is none other than the house of God; this is the gate of heaven" (Genesis 28:16–17).
3. "You will always have the poor among you, but you will not always have me" (John 12:7-8).
4. "Go wash yourself seven times in the Jordan, and your flesh will be restored and you will be cleansed" (2 Kings 5:8–10).
5. "The Holy Spirit will come upon you, and the power of the Most High will overshadow you. So the holy one to be born will be called the Son of God" (Luke 1:35).
6. "The voice is the voice of Jacob, but the hands are the hands of Esau" (Genesis 27:22).
7. "If the world hates you, keep in mind that it hated me first" (John 15:18).

All Your Heart

Love the Lord your God with all your heart...
(**Jesus,** *in* MATTHEW *22:37)*

UNLOCK THE TREASURE BOX:

What's the KEY WORD *(it goes where you see the* ***) in this passage?

____
* * *

(It begins with the letter "H")

"The good man brings good things out of the good stored up in his ***, and the evil man brings evil things out of the evil stored up in his ***. For out of the overflow of his *** the mouth speaks."

— Jesus, in LUKE **6:45**

Love the Lord your God...with all your mind...
*(**Jesus,** in MATTHEW 22:37)*

SWORD-SHARPENERS—"The sword of the Spirit...is the word of God" (EPHESIANS 6:17). For each verse below, fill in the right word at the beginning — at the "tip of the sword." (When you read down, the first letters of these words will spell the word MIND.)

"M_______ plans by seeking advice" (PROVERBS 20:18).

"I_______ we are out of our mind, it is for the sake of God" (2 CORINTHIANS 5:13).

"N_______ one whose hope is in you will ever be put to shame" (PSALM 25:3).

"D_______ your son and he will give you peace; he will bring delight to your soul" (PROVERBS 29:17).

Don't know an ANSWER? Look first in the Bible, then in the back of this book...

Jesus Our King

He is Lord of lords and King of kings—and with him will be his called, chosen and faithful followers. (Revelation 17:14)

THE KING'S WORDS—Who did Jesus make each of these statements to?

1. "Go to the lake and throw out your line. Take the first fish you catch; open its mouth and you will find a four-drachma coin. Take it and give it to them for my tax and yours" (Matthew 17:27).
2. "You would have no power over me if it were not given to you from above. Therefore the one who handed me over to you is guilty of a greater sin" (John 19:11).
3. "Do you truly love me more than these?" (John 21:15).

4. "I hold this against you: You have forsaken your first love" (REVELATION 2:4).

5. "Be faithful, even to the point of death, and I will give you the crown of life" (REVELATION 2:10).

6. "I know where you live—where Satan has his throne. Yet you remain true to my name" (REVELATION 2:13).

7. "I have this against you: You tolerate that woman Jezebel, who calls herself a prophetess" (REVELATION 2:20).

8. "I know your deeds; you have a reputation of being alive, but you are dead. Wake up! Strengthen what remains and is about to die, for I have not found your deeds complete in the sight of my God" (REVELATION 3:1-2).

9. "I know your deeds. See, I have placed before you an open door that no one can shut. I know that you have little strength, yet you have kept my word and have not denied my name" (REVELATION 3:8).

10. "Because you are lukewarm—neither hot nor cold—I am about to spit you out of my mouth. You say, 'I am rich; I have acquired wealth and do not need a thing.' But you do not realize that you are wretched, pitiful, poor, blind and naked" (REVELATION 3:16-17)

Don't know an ANSWER? Look first in the Bible, then in the back of this book...

God's People

You are a chosen people, a royal priesthood, a holy nation, a people belonging to God. (1 PETER 2:9)

NAME CHANGE: These people were given new names in the Bible. Their old names are listed here; what were their new names?

1. *Abram* (GENESIS 17:5) (Who changed Abram's name?)
2. *Sarai* (GENESIS 17:15) (Who changed Sarai's name?)
3. *Jacob* (GENESIS 32:28) (Who changed Jacob's name?)
4. *Simon* the fisherman (MARK 3:16, JOHN 1:42) (Who changed Simon's name?)

▼ ▼ ▼

5. Saul of Tarsus also became known by another name. What was it? (ACTS 13:9)

A FAMILY BECOMES GOD'S PEOPLE—

6. The man who was the father of God's people went to live near the great trees of Mamre. What was his name? (GENESIS 13:18, 18:1)
7. When this man and his wife were very old, they had a son. What was the son's name? (GENESIS 21:1–7)
8. This son then grew up and had two sons who were twins. The first twin was hairy and had reddish skin. What was his name? (GENESIS 25:21–25)
9. What was the second twin's name? (GENESIS 25:26)
10. The second son had twelve sons of his own. Can you name all twelve (in any order)? (GENESIS 35:23–26)

★★★ The Promised Land

Then the Lord said, "This is the land I promised on oath to Abraham, Isaac and Jacob." (Deuteronomy 34:4)

MOSES GETS A LOOK AT THE PROMISED LAND—

1. One day, God told Moses to climb a high mountain, and to look from a distance at the land He was giving to the people of Israel. What was the name of this mountain? **(Deuteronomy 32:48-52)**
2. What else would happen to Moses on this mountain? **(32:50)**

Earlier that day, Moses spoke the words about God's Law that you see below **(32:47)**. Supply the missing words from the list:

"They are not just idle words for you—they are your (3) ______. By them you will live (4) ______ in the (5) ______ you are crossing the Jordan to possess."

land long life

WHICH WAY?—
If you were starting a trip from Jerusalem back in Bible times, which direction would you go to get to these places? Match each place name to an arrow on the map.

PLACES: *Red Sea* *Damascus* *Philistia* *Jericho* *Mount Carmel* *Moab* *Bethany*

1. ____________
2. ____________
3. ____________

JERUSALEM

7. ____________
4. ____________

6. ____________
5. ____________

N

Talking with God

*Ask and it will be given to you; seek and you will find; knock and the door will be opened to you. (**Jesus,** in MATTHEW 7:7)*

SWORD-SHARPENERS—"The sword of the Spirit...is the word of God" (EPHESIANS 6:17). For each verse below, fill in the right word at the beginning — at the "tip of the sword." (When you read down, the first letters of these words will spell the word PRAY.)

"P_______ be to the Lord, for he has heard my cry for mercy" (PSALM 28:6).

"R_______ me, O Lord, when you show favor to your people, come to my aid when you save them" (PSALM 106:4).

"A_______ the earth bows down to you; they sing praise to you, they sing praise to your name" (PSALM 66:4).

"Y_______ are awesome, O God, in your sanctuary" (PSALM 68:35).

EXTRA EXERCISE—***Keep your Bible handy!***

EVEN MORE GREAT STARTS — Name the book that begins with each of these verses:

1. After the death of Saul, David returned from defeating the Amalekites and stayed in Ziklag two days.
2. In the days when the judges ruled, there was a famine in the land, and a man from Bethlehem in Judah, together with his wife and two sons, went to live for a while in the country of Moab.
3. A record of the genealogy of Jesus Christ the son of David, the son of Abraham. Abraham was the father of Isaac, Isaac the father of Jacob,...
4. After the death of Joshua, the Israelites asked the Lord, "Who will be the first to go up and fight for us against the Canaanites?"
5. How deserted lies the city, once so full of people! How like a widow is she, who once was great among the nations!
6. The word of the Lord came to Jonah son of Amittai: "Go to the great city of Nineveh and preach against it, because its wickedness has come up before me."
7. The elder, to the chosen lady and her children, whom I love in the truth.

Honey from the comb is sweet to your taste.
Know also that wisdom is sweet to your soul. (PROVERBS 24:13-14)

ABC's—Words that start with each letter of the alphabet will complete these verses from **PROVERBS**, the wisdom book. Use the clue that follows each letter to find the missing word.

A— (CLUE:) *Pets, and other creatures like them;* (VERSE:) "A good man takes care of his a__________" (12:10).

B— *A whipping;* "A fool's words start quarrels. They make people want to give him a b__________" (18:6).

C— *A circle of precious metals and gems worn upon a ruler's head;* "A good wife is like a c__________ for her husband" (12:4).

D— *Lying;* "Good people will be guided by honesty. But d__________ will destroy those who are not trustworthy" (11:3).

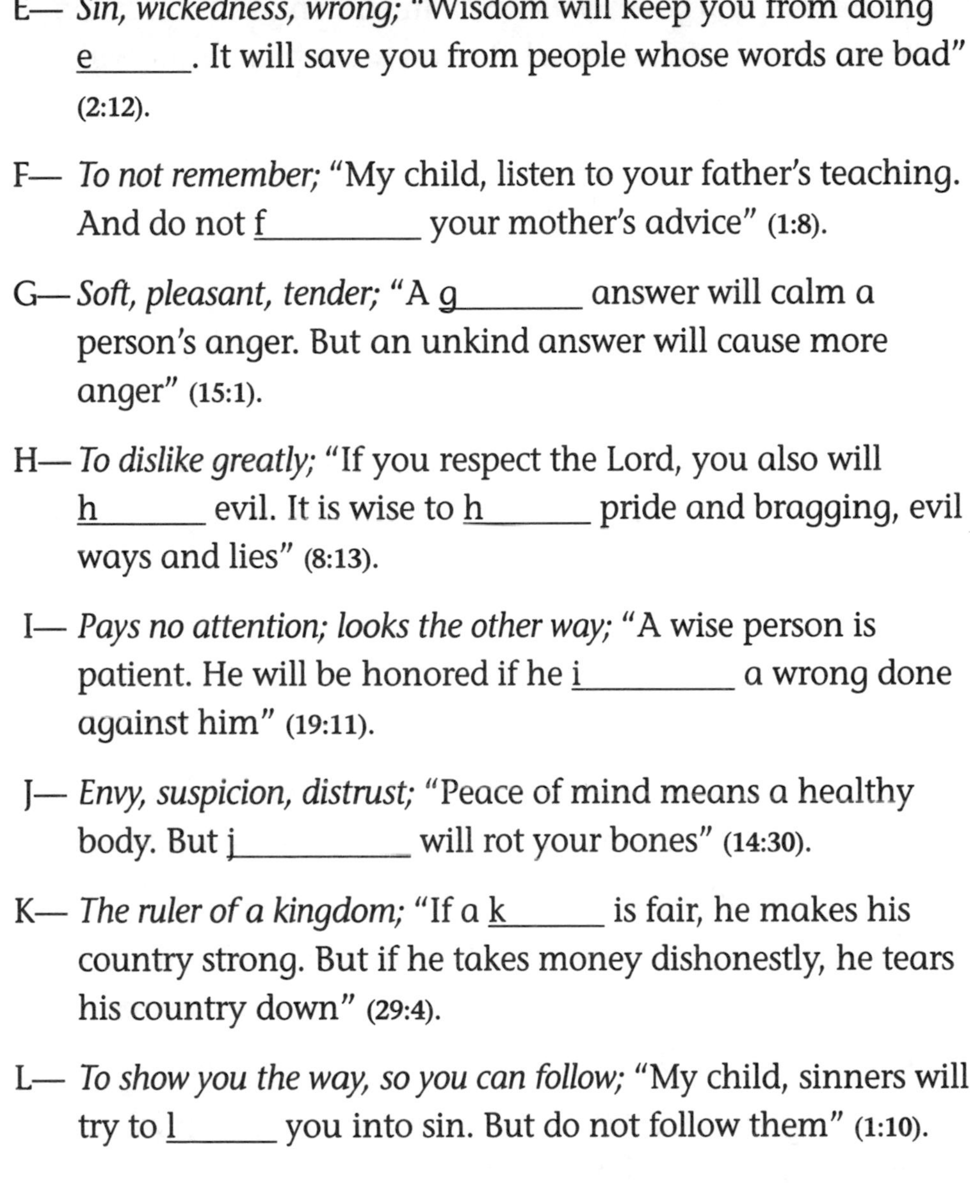

E— *Sin, wickedness, wrong;* "Wisdom will keep you from doing e______. It will save you from people whose words are bad" (2:12).

F— *To not remember;* "My child, listen to your father's teaching. And do not f__________ your mother's advice" (1:8).

G— *Soft, pleasant, tender;* "A g________ answer will calm a person's anger. But an unkind answer will cause more anger" (15:1).

H— *To dislike greatly;* "If you respect the Lord, you also will h_______ evil. It is wise to h_______ pride and bragging, evil ways and lies" (8:13).

I— *Pays no attention; looks the other way;* "A wise person is patient. He will be honored if he i__________ a wrong done against him" (19:11).

J— *Envy, suspicion, distrust;* "Peace of mind means a healthy body. But j___________ will rot your bones" (14:30).

K— *The ruler of a kingdom;* "If a k_______ is fair, he makes his country strong. But if he takes money dishonestly, he tears his country down" (29:4).

L— *To show you the way, so you can follow;* "My child, sinners will try to l______ you into sin. But do not follow them" (1:10).

CONTINUED ON NEXT PAGE

M—*The woman who gave you birth;* "Punishment and correction make a child wise. If he is left to do as he pleases, he will disgrace his m__________" (29:15).

N—*Not anything;* "Whoever brings trouble to his family will be left with n__________ but the wind" (11:29).

O—*A liquid that you can heat and cook food in;* "Wise people store up the best foods and olive o______. But a foolish person eats up everything he has" (21:20).

P—*Having very little money, or the things money can buy;* "A lazy person will end up p________. But a hard worker will become rich" (10:4).

Q—*Not talking loudly;* "A person without good sense finds fault with his neighbor. But a person with understanding keeps q__________" (11:12).

R—*Reverence; awe; honor; worshipful fear;* "Knowledge begins with r__________ for the Lord. But foolish people hate wisdom and self-control" (1:7).

S—*The daughter of your mother and father;* "Be good to wisdom as if she were your s__________. Make understanding your closest friend" (7:4).

T—*Something very valuable;* "Search for wisdom as you would for silver. Hunt for it like hidden t__________" (2:4).

U— *Not punished;* "Be sure of this: The wicked will not go u________, but those who are righteous will go free" (11:21).

V— *Great worth, high price;* "Believe in the v________ of wisdom, and it will make you great. Use it, and it will bring honor to you" (4:8).

W—*Riches, possessions;* "Honor the Lord by giving him part of your w________. Give him the firstfruits from all your crops" (3:9).

X— *The number after five;* "There are ____x things the Lord hates. There are seven things he cannot stand: a proud look, a lying tongue, hands that kill innocent people, a mind that thinks up evil plans, feet that are quick to do evil, a witness who tells lies, and a man who causes trouble among brothers" (6:16–19).

Y— *The person who's reading this page right now;* "The Lord sees everything y____ do. He watches where y____ go" (5:21).

Z— *Surprising, wonderful;* "There are three things that are too ____zing for me, four that I do not understand: the way of an eagle in the sky, the way of a snake on a rock, the way of a ship on the high seas, and the way of a man with a maiden" (30:18-19).

*"The Holy Spirit...will teach you all things and will remind you of everything I have said to you." (**Jesus,** in* JOHN *14:26)*

SEARCH AND ENJOY: FIND THE FRUIT—In Galatians 5:22-23 we read about nine qualities or virtues which are called "the fruit of the Spirit." The Holy Spirit builds these qualities into our lives. *We must have His help to fully know and enjoy these qualities!*

The search-exercise on the following pages will give you the name of each of these nine virtues, in the correct order. Below each numbered answer space, you'll find two verses. In both of these verses, a quality or virtue which is one of the fruits of the Spirit is listed. As you find the quality which is repeated in both verses in each set, you'll have the full list of "the fruits of the Spirit." *(Remember:* Each correct answer is included in *both* of the verses in each set.)

1. ____________________

Over all these virtues put on love... (COLOSSIANS 3:14)

Whoever lives in love lives in God... (1 JOHN 4:16)

2. ____________________

Shout for joy to the Lord, all the earth... (PSALM 100:1)

Indeed, you are our glory and joy... (1 THESSALONIANS 2:20)

3. ____________________

Mercy, peace, and love be yours in abundance... (JUDE 1:2)

Righteousness, peace, and joy in the Holy Spirit... (ROMANS 14:17)

CONTINUED ON NEXT PAGE

4. ______________________

A man's wisdom gives him patience... (PROVERBS 19:11)

Patience is better than pride... (ECCLESIASTES 7:8)

5. ______________________

In purity, understanding, patience and kindness... (2 CORINTHIANS 6:6)

Consider the kindness and sternness of God... (ROMANS 11:22)

6. ______________________

Surely goodness and love will follow me... (PSALM 23:6)

What can I repay the Lord for all his goodness to me? (PSALM 116:12)

7. ______________________

Love and faithfulness keep a king safe... (PROVERBS 20:28)

This calls for patient endurance and faithfulness... (REVELATION 13:10)

8. ______________________

Let your gentleness be evident to all... (PHILIPPIANS 4:5)

Do this with gentleness and respect... (1 PETER 3:15)

9. ______________________

Righteousness, self-control, and the judgment to come... (ACTS 24:25)

Like a city whose walls are broken down is a man who lacks self-control... (PROVERBS 25:28)

Love never fails. (1 Corinthians 13:8)

POWER PASSAGE: THE STRENGTH OF LOVE—Complete this favorite passage in 1 Corinthians 13:4-8 by adding the right words in the right places. Choose them from the list of words below.

"Love is (1) p______, love is (2) k______. It does not (3) e______, it does not (4) b______, it is not (5) p______. It is not (6) r______, it is not (7) s______, it is not easily (8) a______, it keeps no record of (9) w______. Love does not delight in (10) e______ but rejoices with the (11) t______. It always (12) p______, always (13) t______, always (14) h______, always (15) p______. Love never (16) f______."

truth protects evil envy angered kind proud rude hopes wrongs self-seeking trusts patient perseveres fails boast

Don't know an ANSWER? Look first in the Bible, then in the back of this book...

And God said, "Let there be lights in the expanse of the sky to separate the day from the night, and let them serve as signs to mark seasons and days and years." (Genesis 1:14)

TIME LINE: Match the following events with the approximate date shown beside the time line on the next page.

1. Eli hears Hannah weeping because she doesn't have any children. (1 Samuel 1)
2. Baby Jacob is grasping Esau's heel as these two twin brothers are born. (Genesis 25:24-26)
3. In Isaiah's vision, an angel flies from God's throne and touches Isaiah's mouth with a burning coal. (Isaiah 6:1-8)

4. A prophet warns Paul that he will be taken prisoner in Jerusalem. (Acts 21:10-11)

5. To guide Israel out of Egypt, God sends a pillar of cloud by day and of fire by night. (Exodus 13:21)

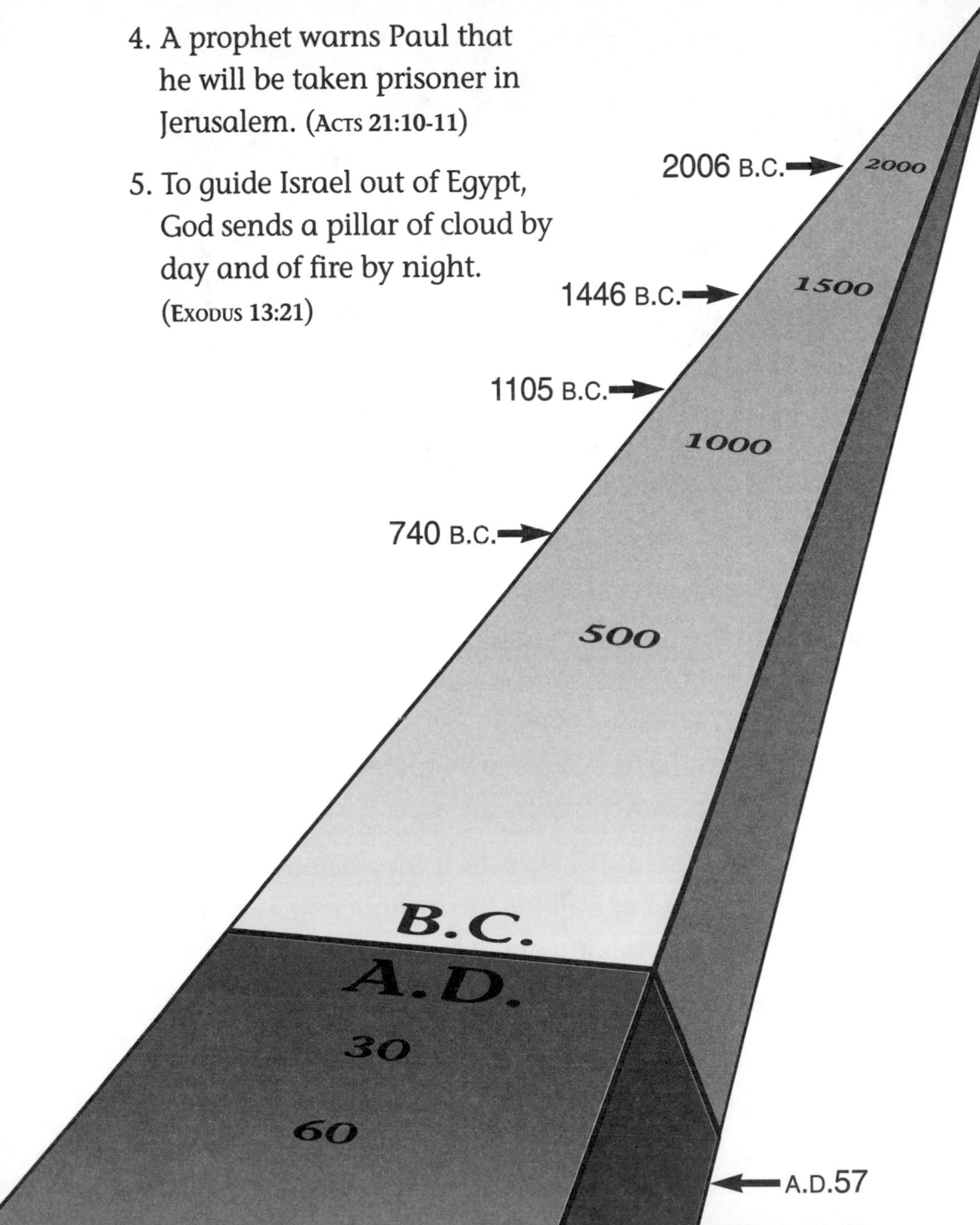

★★★ Jesus Our Savior

Jesus lives forever.... He is always able to save those who come to God through him. (HEBREWS 7:24-25)

FROM SLAVERY TO FREEDOM— Paul reminded the Galatians about the time in their past when they didn't know God: "You were *slaves* to gods that were not real," he said. "But now you know the true God" (GALATIANS 4:8–9).

In the same way, Jesus told some people who didn't believe in Him that "everyone who lives in sin is a *slave* to sin" (JOHN 8:34).

1. Jesus also told these unbelievers that they belonged to someone who is "a liar and the father of lies" (JOHN 8:44). Who is this liar Jesus was talking about?

2. In John 8:36, Jesus told these unbelievers how to escape from their slavery. What missing word is used twice in this verse:

   "If the Son makes you f_______, then you will be truly f_______."

SWORD-SHARPENERS—"The sword of the Spirit...is the word of God" (Ephesians 6:17). For each verse below, fill in the right word at the beginning — at the "tip of the sword." (When you read down, the first letters of these words will spell the word <u>SAVIOR</u>.)

"S________ the Lord while he may be found; call on him while he is near" (Isaiah 55:6).

"A________ the suffering of his soul, he will see the light of life and be satisfied" (Isaiah 53:11).

"V________ early in the morning, the chief priests, with the elders, the teachers of the law and the whole Sanhedrin, reached a decision. They bound Jesus, led him away and handed him over to Pilate" (Mark 15:1).

"I________ is by the name of Jesus Christ of Nazareth, whom you crucified but whom God raised from the dead, that this man stands before you healed" (Acts 4:10).

"O________ of the criminals who hung there hurled insults at him: "Aren't you the Christ? Save yourself and us!" (Luke 23:39).

"R________, let us go! Here comes my betrayer" (Matthew 26:46).

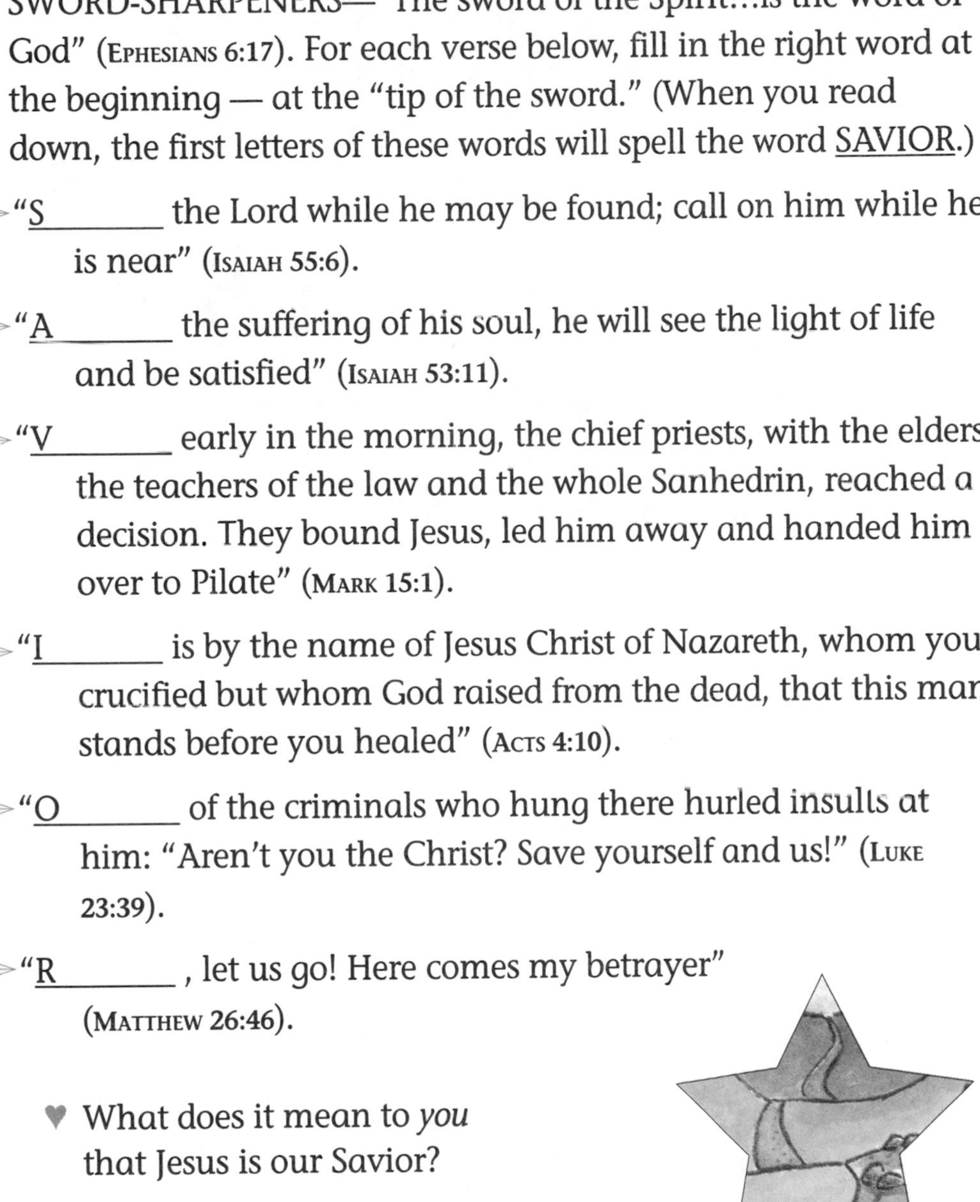

♥ What does it mean to *you* that Jesus is our Savior?

Don't know an ANSWER? Look first in the Bible, then in the back of this book...

Praise be to the Lord my Rock, who trains my hands for war, my fingers for battle. (Psalm 144:1)

FIGHTERS IN THE BOOK OF JUDGES—

1. A left-handed Israelite made a double-edged sword, and strapped it to his thigh under his clothing. In those days the nation of Moab had power over Israel, and Israel had to pay riches to the king of Moab, a fat man named Eglon. The left-handed Israelite stepped before the king to pay the riches. Then he said, "I have a secret message for the king." The king ordered his helpers to leave him. When the left-handed Israelite was alone with the king, he said to him, "I have a message from God for you." He plunged the sword into the king's belly, which was so fat that the sword went completely inside him. Who was this left-handed Israelite? (Judges 3:12-26)

2. With only an oxgoad (a stick used to drive oxen), this man killed 600 Philistines. Who was he? (Judges 3:31)

3. She was brave and bold, and the only woman who led Israel during the time of the Judges. Who was she? (Judges 4—5)

4. The Midianites had power over Israel, and would not let the people have any food. One day a farmer was secretly threshing wheat in a winepress, to keep it from the Midianites. Then an angel appeared to him and said, "The Lord is with you, mighty warrior." This man went on to save Israel from the Midianites. Who was he? (Judges 6—8)

5. This wicked man was Gideon's son, and he killed all but one of his seventy half-brothers. Later he set fire to a tower in Shechem and killed a thousand men and women. When he attacked another tower in Thebez, a woman dropped a stone on his head and cracked his skull. Who was he? (Judges 9)

6. This man, a son of Gilead, was called a "mighty warrior." He was driven away from his home by his brothers, but later his family and neighbors asked him to be their commander and to lead the attack against the Ammonites. Who was he? (Judges 11)

Don't know an ANSWER? Look first in the Bible, then in the back of this book...

Coming Kingdom

I will not drink of this fruit of the vine again until that day when I drink it new with you in my Father's kingdom. (**Jesus,** *in* MATTHEW *26:29*)

UNLOCK THE TREASURE BOX:

What's the KEY WORD *(it goes where you see the* ***) in this passage?

____

* * *

(It begins with the letter "N")

"Then I saw a *** heaven and a *** earth, for the first heaven and the first earth had passed away, and there was no longer any sea. I saw the Holy City, the *** Jerusalem, coming down out of heaven from God.... He who was seated on the throne said, 'I am making everything ***!'"
— REVELATION 21:1-5

Fan the Flame

I remind you to fan into flame the gift of God which is in you.
(2 Timothy 1:6)

1. In 1 Thessalonians 5:19, whose fire are we told not to put out?

Ephesians 4:11 is one of the places in Scripture where we find a list of some of the special gifts God has given to His church—the abilities He has given different people to do different "jobs" in the Church.. Unscramble these letters to learn the names of these "jobs," which are really gifts from God:

2. p s l a o s t e
3. t e s p o h r p
4. a s e l v n e s g i t
5. s o r t a p s *and* c h s t a e e r

Our fight is not against people on earth.... We are fighting against the spiritual powers of evil in the heavenly world. (EPHESIANS 6:12)

FIRE!

1. Who will be thrown into a lake of fire? (**REVELATION 20:7-15**)
2. Whose eyes are like a fire, with a face as bright as the blazing sun? (**REVELATION 1:12-18**)
3. In Mark 9:43 and Matthew 25:41, Jesus spoke about how long the fire of hell will last. How long will it last?
4. The world we live in now will not last forever. We learn in 2 Peter 3:10-12 what will happen to it on "the day of the Lord." What will God use to destroy it?

“ ”

WHO SAID THIS?

Tell who spoke each of these questions or statements in the Bible:

1. “Whether he is a sinner or not, I don’t know. One thing I do know. I was blind but now I see!” (John 9:25).
2. “Where is the one who has been born king of the Jews? We saw his star in the east and have come to worship him” (Matthew 2:1-2).
3. “It is more blessed to give than to receive” (Acts 20:35).
4. “Son, why have you treated us like this? Your father and I have been anxiously searching for you” (Luke 2:48).
5. “If only we had meat to eat! We remember the fish we ate in Egypt at no cost — also the cucumbers, melons, leeks, onions and garlic. But now we have lost our appetite; we never see anything but this manna!” (Numbers 11:4-6).
6. “Did God really say, ‘You must not eat from any tree in the garden’?” (Genesis 3:1).
7. “You snakes! You brood of vipers! How will you escape being condemned to hell?” (Matthew 23:33).
8. “Do you refuse to speak to me? Don’t you realize I have power either to free you or to crucify you?” (John 19:10).
9. “Who is the Lord, that I should obey him and let Israel go? I do not know the Lord and I will not let Israel go” (Exodus 5:2).

Treasure Chest

Store up for yourselves treasures in heaven, where moth and rust do not destroy, and where thieves do not break in and steal.
*(**Jesus,** in MATTHEW 6:20)*

PLANT THE SEEDS—"The seed is the word of God," Jesus said (LUKE 8:11). In each planter-pot, plant the right "seed-word"—the word that makes the verse complete, ready to grow in your heart.

SEED-WORDS: *advice precious time way made above poor wealth*

1. ______________

Good sense is far more valuable than gold or __________ jewels.
(PROVERBS 20:15)

2. ______________

For the value of wisdom is far ________ rubies; nothing can be compared with it.
(PROVERBS 8:11)

3. ______________

I, Wisdom, give good _______ and common sense.... My gifts are better than the purest gold or sterling silver!
(PROVERBS 8:14–19)

4. ______________

Some rich people are poor, and some poor people have great _______!
(PROVERBS 13:7)

5. ______________

A man who loves pleasure becomes poor; wine and luxury are not the _____ to riches!
(PROVERBS 21:17)

6. ______________

Better to be _______ and honest than rich and a cheater.
(PROVERBS 28:6)

7. ______________

Don't weary yourself trying to get rich. Why waste your ______? For riches can disappear as though they had the wings of a bird!
(PROVERBS 23:4)

8. ______________

The rich and the poor are alike before the Lord who ______ them all.
(PROVERBS 22:2)

Don't know an ANSWER? Look first in the Bible, then in the back of this book...

4 ★★★★

Faces and Places

The Sovereign Lord will wipe away the tears from all faces.
(Isaiah 25:8)

WHICH HAPPENED FIRST?

1. God gave a baby to Sarah in her old age, or God gave a baby to Elizabeth in her old age? (Genesis 21:1-7, Luke 1)
2. Cain was born, or Abel was born? (Genesis 4:1–2)
3. Jacob was born, or Esau was born? (Genesis 25:24-26)
4. Abraham's son Isaac was born, or Abraham's son Ishmael was born? (Genesis 16; 21)
5. John the Baptist was born, or Jesus Christ was born? (Luke 1—2)
6. David's son Solomon was born, or David's son Amnon was born? (2 Samuel 3:2, 5:13-14)

FRONTWARD, BACKWARD—The names of the following people can be spelled the same way either frontward or backward (like the name "BOB"). Can you say who they are?

7. This woman had no children. Then she promised God that if He gave her a son, she would give him up to serve in God's house all his life. (1 SAMUEL 1:9–11)

8. This old widow lived in the Temple in Jerusalem. When the parents of baby Jesus brought Him there, she saw Him and gave thanks to God. (LUKE 2:36–37)

9. This king followed God for many years. But then he stopped depending on God's help. He put one of God's prophets in prison, and mistreated some of the people. He would not even ask for God's help after getting a disease in his feet, and he died before reaching old age. (2 CHRONICLES 14—16)

▼ ▼ ▼

10. In 1 Samuel 25 we read about a man whose name meant "fool." Because of his foolish actions he almost got himself killed by David. In Genesis 29—31 we read about an another often selfish man who was Jacob's father-in-law. You can take each of these two men's name's, spell it backward, and it becomes the <u>other</u> man's name. What are their names?

♥ What does *your* name spell backwards?

Don't know an ANSWER? Look first in the Bible, then in the back of this book...

Jesus Our Friend

I have called you friends, for everything that I learned from my Father I have made known to you. (**Jesus**, *in* JOHN *15:15*)

UNLOCK THE TREASURE BOX:

What's the KEY WORD *(it goes where you see the* ***) in this passage?

____

* * *

(It begins with the letter "L")

"God is *** . This is how God showed his *** among us: He sent his one and only Son into the world that we might live through him. This is *** : not that we ***d God, but that he ***d us and sent his Son as an atoning sacrifice for our sins."

—1 JOHN 4:8-10

NAMES OF JESUS—Here are some of the names Jesus used for Himself. All of these on this page are found in the gospel of John. Match each one with the right verse from John below.

The Way and the Truth and the Life
The Resurrection and the Life *The Vine*
Bread of Life *Light of the World* *Good Shepherd*

1. "I am the _______________. He who comes to me will never go hungry, and he who believes in me will never be thirsty" (6:35).
2. "I am the _______________. Whoever follows me will never walk in darkness, but will have the light of life" (8:12).
3. "I am the _______________. I know my sheep and my sheep know me—just as the Father knows me and I know the Father—and I lay down my life for the sheep" (10:14–15).
4. "I am _______________. He who believes in me will live, even though he dies" (11:25).
5. "I am _______________. No one comes to the Father except through me" (14:6).
6. "I am _______________; you are the branches. If a man remains in me and I in him, he will bear much fruit; apart from me you can do nothing" (15:5).

They were brave warriors, ready for battle... Their faces were the faces of lions...they were as swift as gazelles in the mountains. (1 CHRONICLES 12:8)

WHICH HAPPENED FIRST?

1. Stephen was killed in Jerusalem, or Jesus was killed in Jerusalem? (JOHN 19, ACTS 7)
2. Peter and John healed a crippled man, or Jesus healed a crippled woman? (LUKE 13:10-17, ACTS 3:1-10)
3. The prophet Elijah raised a widow's son to life, or Jesus raised a widow's son to life? (1 KINGS 17:17-24, LUKE 7:11-16)
4. The prophet Elisha healed a man of leprosy, or Jesus healed a man of leprosy? (2 KINGS 5:1-14, MARK 1:40-45)
5. Paul healed the father of a Roman official in Malta, or Jesus healed the servant of a Roman centurion? (MATTHEW 8:5-13, ACTS 28:7-8)

6. Before the battle of Jericho, Joshua said that only one family in the city was to be kept alive after Israel took the city. Whose family was this? (JOSHUA 6:17)
7. Joshua sent only part of his army to capture the city of Ai. But because one of the soldiers of Israel had disobeyed God, the people of Ai beat them back. Who was this man who sinned? (JOSHUA 7)
8. Israel again went to capture Ai. This time Joshua split his army into two groups. One group went by night behind the city. Joshua led the other group in front of the city, and in the morning all the men of Ai came out to fight. Joshua and his men pretended to retreat, and the men of Ai came after them. But when they looked back at their city, what did they see? (JOSHUA 8:20)
9. After the battle of Ai, Joshua built an altar to the Lord on Mount Ebal. There on the altar he sacrificed burnt offerings to God, and he also read something aloud to the people of Israel. What did he read to them? (JOSHUA 8:34-35)
10. In the battle of Gibeon against the five Amorite kings, Joshua prayed a prayer, and something happened to the sun. What was it? (JOSHUA 10:1-15)
11. While their armies were being defeated in the battle of Gibeon, the five Amorite kings ran away and hid in a cave. Joshua was still busy with the battle, but what did he do so these five kings would not escape? (JOSHUA 10:16-28)

Don't know an ANSWER? Look first in the Bible, then in the back of this book…

THE VOICE OF GOD

Each of these statements was spoken in the Scriptures by God. For each one, tell who God was speaking to.

1. "Your brother's blood cries out to me from the ground. Now you are under a curse and driven from the ground, which opened its mouth to receive your brother's blood from your hand. When you work the ground, it will no longer yield its crops for you. You will be a restless wanderer on the earth" (GENESIS 4:10-12).
2. "Go to the house of Judas on Straight Street and ask for a man from Tarsus named Saul, for he is praying. In a vision he has seen a man named Ananias come and place his hands on him to restore his sight" (ACTS 9:11-12).
3. "Go and present yourself to Ahab, and I will send rain on the land" (1 KINGS 18:1).
4. "Go back to the land of your fathers and to your relatives, and I will be with you" (GENESIS 31:3).
5. "Do not be afraid to go down to Egypt, for I will make you into a great nation there. I will go down to Egypt with you, and I will surely bring you back again. And Joseph's own hand will close your eyes" (GENESIS 46:1-4).
6. "See, I am about to do something in Israel that will make the ears of everyone who hears of it tingle" (1 SAMUEL 3:11).

The Lord is faithful to all his promises. (PSALM 145:13)

PROMISE POWER—Match the right ending *(from the list below)* to each of these powerful promises in God's Word.

1. This is the confidence we have in approaching God: that if we ask anything according to his will,...
2. He who began a good work in you...
3. The Lord is faithful,...

(A)• *and he will strengthen and protect you from the evil one* (2 THESSALONIANS 3:3).

(B)• *will carry it on to completion until the day of Christ Jesus* (PHILIPPIANS 1:6).

(C)• *he hears us* (1 JOHN 5:14).

Don't know an ANSWER? Look first in the Bible, then in the back of this book...

I will remember the deeds of the Lord; yes, I will remember your miracles of long ago. (PSALM 77:11)

MIRACLES—WHY AND WHY NOT?

1. According to what God told Moses in Exodus 3:18-20, why did God have to bring down the plagues upon Egypt?
2. The Pharisees and teachers of the law came to Jesus and said, "Teacher, we want to see a miraculous sign from you." Did Jesus show them a sign? (**MATTHEW 12:38-42, 16:1-4**)
3. In John 6:14-15, we read of a time when some people who had seen the miracles of Jesus wanted to make Him a king. So what did Jesus do?
4. God gave Moses the power to throw his staff to the ground, and have it turn into a snake. Why did God say He was letting Moses do this? (**EXODUS 4:1-5**)

A WEEK'S WORK—Below are listed the things God made in the week of Creation that we read about in Genesis 1. Match them up with the right day on which they were made.

birds dry ground fish land animals light man
moon oceans plants sky stars sun trees

5. On the FIRST Day of Creation, God made: ___________
6. On the SECOND Day of Creation, God made: ___________
7. On the THIRD Day of Creation, God made:

___________ ___________ ___________ ___________

8. On the FOURTH Day of Creation, God made:

___________ ___________ ___________

9. On the FIFTH Day of Creation, God made:

___________ ___________

10. On the SIXTH Day of Creation, God made:

___________ ___________

And on the SEVENTH Day,
God rested from His work.

Don't know an ANSWER? Look first in the Bible, then in the back of this book...

Knowing God

We will not fear even if the oceans roar and foam, or if the mountains shake at the raging sea.... God says, "Be quiet and know that I am God." (PSALM 46:3-10)

1. In Exodus 33:11, we read that the Lord would speak to this man "face to face, as a man speaks with his friend." Who was this man?
2. In 1 Kings 19:9–18, we read about God sending Elijah out to stand on a mountain and meet Him. Then there came...

a *windstorm,*

an *earthquake,*

a *fire,*

and the sound of a *gentle whisper.*

But God was in only one of these that day. Which was it?

Jesus taught us what God is like—not only by how He lived, but also in what He said about God.

3. To whom did Jesus say these words: "God is spirit"? (John 4:24)
4. To whom did Jesus say, "He is not the God of the dead but of the living"? (Matthew 22:32)
5. To whom did Jesus say, "All things are possible with God"? (Mark 10:27)
6. To whom did Jesus say, "God knows your hearts. What is highly valued among men is detestable in God's sight"? (Luke 16:15)
7. To whom did Jesus say, "It is easier for a camel to go through the eye of a needle than for a rich man to enter the kingdom of God"? (Luke 18:23-25)
8. To whom did Jesus say, "For God so loved the world that he gave his one and only Son, that whoever believes in him shall not perish but have eternal life"? (John 3:16)
9. To whom did Jesus say, "My Father is always at his work to this very day, and I, too, am working"? (John 5:17)

♥ What new things are you learning about God in *your* life?

I tell you the truth, no one can see the kingdom of God unless he is born again. (***Jesus***, *in* JOHN *3:3*)

UNLOCK THE TREASURE BOX:

What's the KEY WORD *(it goes where you see the ****) in this passage?

______

* * *

(It begins with the letter "P")

"*** the Lord. *** the Lord from the heavens, *** him in the heights above. *** him, all his angels, *** him, all his heavenly hosts. *** him, sun and moon, *** him, all you shining stars. *** him, you highest heavens and you waters above the skies. Let them *** the name of the Lord."

— PSALM 148:1-5

WHO SAID THIS?

Tell who spoke each of these questions or statements in the Bible:

1. "You intended to harm me, but God intended it for good to accomplish what is now being done, the saving of many lives. So then, don't be afraid. I will provide for you and your children" (GENESIS 50:19-21).
2. "Which one do you want me to release to you: Barabbas, or Jesus who is called Christ?" (MATTHEW 27:17).
3. "I urge you to keep up your courage, because not one of you will be lost; only the ship will be destroyed. Last night an angel of the God whose I am and whom I serve stood beside me and said, 'Do not be afraid, Paul. You must stand trial before Caesar; and God has graciously given you the lives of all who sail with you.' So keep up your courage, men, for I have faith in God that it will happen just as he told me. Nevertheless, we must run aground on some island" (ACTS 27:21-26).
4. "What are you willing to give me if I hand him over to you?" (MATTHEW 26:14-16).
5. "May my lord pay no attention to that wicked man Nabal. He is just like his name—his name is Fool, and folly goes with him" (1 SAMUEL 25:25).
6. "Rabbi, who sinned, this man or his parents, that he was born blind?" (JOHN 9:2).

The name of the Lord is a strong tower; the righteous run to it and are safe. (Proverbs 18:10)

SCRIPTURE SCRAMBLE: Rearrange the words in each numbered sentence below so that the verses read correctly.

1. *not ashamed I of gospel the am power because it the of is God everyone for salvation who of believes... the*

   Romans 1:16

2. *brothers, joy, Consider it my pure trials face whenever you many of kinds.*

   James 1:2

FAMOUS QUESTIONS

WHO ASKED THIS?—Tell who asked each one of these questions in the Bible:

1. "Who is this uncircumcised Philistine that he should defy the armies of the living God?" (1 Samuel 17:26).
2. "What is truth?" (John 18:38).
3. "Who told you that you were naked? Have you eaten from the tree that I commanded you not to eat from?" (Genesis 3:11).
4. "Who am I, that I should go to Pharaoh and bring the Israelites out of Egypt?" (Exodus 3:11).
5. "Lord, how many times shall I forgive my brother when he sins against me? Up to seven times?" (Matthew 18:21).
6. "John's baptism—where did it come from? Was it from heaven, or from men?" (Matthew 21:25).
7. "Why wasn't this perfume sold and the money given to the poor?" (John 12:4-5).
8. "Are you greater than our father Jacob, who gave us the well and drank from it himself, as did also his sons and his flocks and herds?" (John 4:12).
9. "How can a man be born when he is old?" (John 3:4).
10. "Lord, are you going to wash my feet?" (John 13:6).

Bible Numbers

*How precious to me are your thoughts, O God!
How vast is the sum of them! Were I to count them,
they would outnumber the grains of sand.* (PSALM 139:17-18)

NOAH NUMBERS: You'll find the answers for the following questions in chapters 6—9 of the book of Genesis.

1. How many sons did Noah have? (GENESIS 6:10)

For building the ark the right size, God gave Noah the measurements in *cubits* (6:15). The three main measurements were:

300 cubits *50 cubits* *30 cubits*

2. Which measurement was for how *long* the ark would be?
3. Which measurement was for how *high* the ark would be?
4. Which measurement was for how *wide* the ark would be?

5. How old was Noah when the floodwaters came on the earth —60 years old, 160 years old, or 600 years old? (7:6)

6. How many of each "clean" animal (animals used for sacrifice) did Noah take with him on the ark? (7:2)

7. How many of each "unclean" animal (animals not used for sacrifice) did Noah take with him on the ark? (7:2)

8. For how many days and nights did rain fall upon the earth? (7:4, 7:12)

9. How many people were on Noah's ark? (7:13)

CONTINUED ON NEXT PAGE

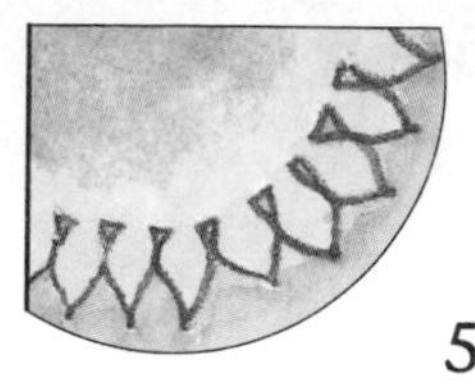

10. After the flood began, how long did it take before the waters went down enough for the ark to rest on a mountaintop—50 days, 150 days, or 500 days? (8:3)

11. After the ark was settled on the mountain, how long did Noah wait before he sent out a raven—40 days, 140 days, or 400 days? (8:6)

12. Noah then sent out a dove, and the dove came back. How long did Noah wait before he sent out the dove again—7 days, 17 days, or 70 days? (8:10)

13. The dove came back this time with a freshly plucked olive leaf in its beak. How long did Noah wait before he sent out the dove again—7 days, 17 days, or 70 days? (8:12)

14. From the day Noah entered the ark until the day he walked out, how long was it—just over 6 months, just over 9 months, or just over 12 months? (7:11–13, 8:13–18)

15. After the flood, how long did Noah live — 30 years, 50 years, or 350 years? (9:28)

16. How old was Noah when he died—630 years, 650 years, or 950 years? (9:29)

When Tough Times Come

Some were laughed at and beaten. Others were tied and put into prison. They were killed with stones and they were cut in half. (Hebrews 11:36-37)

UNLOCK THE TREASURE BOX:

What's the KEY WORD *(it goes where you see the* ***) in this passage?

______
* * *

(It begins with the letter "S")

"For it is commendable if a man bears up under the pain of unjust ***ing because he is conscious of God.... If you *** for doing good and you endure it, this is commendable before God. To this you were called, because Christ ***ed for you, leaving you an example, that you should follow in his steps.... When he ***ed, he made no threats." — 1 Peter 2:19-23

Don't know an ANSWER? Look first in the Bible, then in the back of this book...

Children are a gift from the Lord. (Psalm 127:3)

FAMILY MATCHUP: BROTHER AND BROTHER—From this list of men, match each one with the name of his brother in the numbered list below. And imagine what it was like when they were children growing up together.

Abraham   David   Joab   Jesus

1. Abishai and Asahel (2 Samuel 2:18)
2. Eliab, Abinadab, and Shammah (1 Samuel 17:12-15)
3. James, Joseph, Simon, and Judas (Matthew 13:53-57)
4. Nahor and Haran (Genesis 11:27)

WORDS FROM THE YOUNG—Tell who made each of these statements in the Scriptures:

5. "Shall I go and get one of the Hebrew women to nurse the baby for you?" (Exodus 2:7).
6. "If only my master would see the prophet who is in Samaria! He would cure him of his leprosy" (2 Kings 5:2-3).
7. "The fire and wood are here, but where is the lamb for the burnt offering?" (Genesis 22:7).
8. "Go on up, you baldhead! Go on up, you baldhead!" (2 Kings 2:23).
9. "Here I am; you called me" (1 Samuel 3:5).
10. "Speak, for your servant is listening" (1 Samuel 3:10).
11. "My head! My head!" (2 Kings 4:19).
12. "The Jews have agreed to ask you to bring Paul before the Sanhedrin tomorrow on the pretext of wanting more accurate information about him. Don't give in to them, because more than forty of them are waiting in ambush for him. They have taken an oath not to eat or drink until they have killed him. They are ready now, waiting for your consent to their request" (Acts 23:20-21).

Many women do noble things.... A woman who respects the Lord should be praised. (PROVERBS 31:29-30)

1. After her husband and her two sons had died, she said, "Call me Mara." The word *Mara* means "bitter." But her actual name means "pleasant." Who was she? (**RUTH 1:20**)

2. As she lay dying, her last words were to name her newborn son "Ben-Oni," which means "son of my trouble." But he was later called Benjamin. Who was his mother? (**GENESIS 35:16–18**)

▼ ▼ ▼

3. Eve's name means "Living." Who gave Eve this name? (**GENESIS 3:20**)

4. Why was this name given to her? (**GENESIS 3:20**)

★ GOLD STAR SPECIAL ★

MORE STRONG FINISHES — Name the Old Testament book that ends with each of these verses:

1. They took down the bodies of Saul and his sons from the wall of Beth Shan and went to Jabesh, where they burned them. Then they took their bones and buried them under a tamarisk tree at Jabesh, and they fasted seven days.
2. See, I will send you the prophet Elijah before that great and dreadful day of the Lord comes. He will turn the hearts of the fathers to their children, and the hearts of the children to their fathers; or else I will come and strike the land with a curse.
3. Nothing can heal your wound; your injury is fatal. Everyone who hears the news about you claps his hands at your fall, for who has not felt your endless cruelty?
4. Mordecai the Jew was second in rank to King Xerxes, preeminent among the Jews, and held in high esteem by his many fellow Jews, because he worked for the good of his people and spoke up for the welfare of all the Jews.
5. Nineveh has more than a hundred and twenty thousand people who cannot tell their right hand from their left, and many cattle as well. Should I not be concerned about that great city?

You should recognize the value of men like these.
(1 Corinthians 16:18)

DISCIPLE DRILL: For the following questions, each answer is the name of one or more of the twelve men who made up Jesus' team of disciples. (Some names are used more than once.)

1. Jesus once asked him three times, "Do you love me?" (John 21:15–17)
2. When Jesus went to Gethsemane to pray the night before He was killed, He took these three disciples with Him, and told them to keep watch. (Mark 14:32-34)
3. This man told his brother, "We have found the Messiah" (that is, the Christ). And he brought his brother to Jesus. (John 1:40–42)
4. This disciple was the son of Alphaeus, and he had the same name as the disciple who was John's brother. (Matthew 10:3)

5. Some people in a Samaritan village would not welcome Jesus and the disciples. So two of the disciples said, "Lord, do you want us to call fire down from heaven to destroy them?" But Jesus turned and rebuked them. Which two men said this? (LUKE 9:51-56)
6. This disciple wrote three letters in our New Testament, and all three are called by his name.
7. This disciple was also called "Didymus." Both his names mean "Twin." (JOHN 11:16)
8. Jesus once told him, "Feed my lambs…take care of my sheep…feed my sheep…" (JOHN 21:15-17)
9. This disciple was from Bethsaida, a fishing town on the Sea of Galilee which was also the home of Peter and Andrew. (JOHN 1:44)
10. After meeting Jesus, Philip went to find this man. He said to him, "We have found the one Moses wrote about in the Law, and about whom the prophets also wrote—Jesus of Nazareth." Then this man answered, "Nazareth! Can anything good come from there?" Who was he? (JOHN 1:46)
11. Jesus went to have dinner in this disciple's house. Many tax collectors and "sinners" were there, and the Pharisees didn't like it. (MATTHEW 9:10-11)
12. This disciple preached a great sermon in Jerusalem on the day of Pentecost, and three thousand people became Christians that day. (ACTS 2:14-41)

Our Home in Heaven

Our homeland is in heaven, and we are waiting for our Savior, the Lord Jesus Christ, to come from heaven. (PHILIPPIANS 3:20)

1. This man was Noah's great-grandfather, and he lived on earth for 365 years. The Bible says he "walked with God." Then, instead of dying, God came and took him away to heaven. What was his name? (GENESIS 5:21-24, HEBREWS 11:5)

2. A great prophet also was taken away by God without having to die. God sent a flaming chariot and horses to take him to heaven, and they lifted him up in a whirlwind. Who was he? (2 KINGS 2:11-12)

3. When Jesus was lifted up to heaven, His team of disciples was on the Mount of Olives, watching. What did they see? (ACTS 1:7–12)

WHO SAID THIS?

Tell who spoke each of these statements or questions in the Bible:

1. "Pick me up and throw me into the sea, and it will become calm. I know that it is my fault that this great storm has come upon you" (Jonah 1:12).
2. "Lord, if you had been here, my brother would not have died. But I know that even now God will give you whatever you ask" (John 11:21-22).
3. "If you do not do what is right, sin is crouching at your door; it desires to have you, but you must master it" (Genesis 4:7).
4. "We have no king but Caesar" (John 19:15).
5. "Do not be afraid, for I know that you are looking for Jesus, who was crucified. He is not here; he has risen, just as he said" (Matthew 28:5-6).
6. "If any one of you is without sin, let him be the first to throw a stone at her" (John 8:7).
7. "Master, we've worked hard all night and haven't caught anything. But because you say so, I will let down the nets" (Luke 5:5).
8. "What am I to do with these people? They are almost ready to stone me" (Exodus 17:4).
9. "Today this scripture is fulfilled in your hearing" (Luke 4:21).

Book, Chapter & Verse

These words are like nails that have been driven in firmly. They are wise teachings that come from God the Shepherd. (ECCLESIASTES 12:11)

WHICH BOOK in the Bible…

1. tells about Elijah?—**Genesis, 1 Kings**, or **Judges?**
2. tells about the Good Samaritan—**Matthew, Luke**, or **Romans?**
3. tells about Jesus washing the disciples' feet—**Matthew, Luke**, or **John?**
4. tells about Deborah—**2 Kings, Judges**, or **Esther?**
5. tells about the "valley of dry bones"—**Nehemiah, Ezekiel**, or **Jeremiah?**
6. tells about three men thrown into a furnace of fire—**2 Samuel, Isaiah**, or **Daniel?**
7. tells the most about faith—**Proverbs, Jude**, or **Hebrews?**

TWO-EIGHT—Each of the passages below is verse 8 of chapter 2 in one of the books of the Bible. Can you tell <u>which book</u> each verse is from? (If you need help, refer to the book names listed on the next page.)

8. And there were shepherds living out in the fields nearby, keeping watch over their flocks at night.
9. Then he took a piece of broken pottery and scraped himself with it as he sat among the ashes.
10. Before the spies lay down for the night, she went up on the roof and said to them, "I know that the Lord has given this land to you and that a great fear of you has fallen on us, so that all who live in this country are melting in fear because of you."
11. So Boaz said to her, "My daughter, listen to me. Don't go and glean in another field and don't go away from here. Stay here with my servant girls."
12. He sent them to Bethlehem and said, "Go and make a careful search for the child. As soon as you find him, report to me, so that I may go and worship him."
13. Yet I am writing you a new command; its truth is seen in him and you, because the darkness is passing and the true light is already shining.
14. Their land is full of idols; they bow down to the work of their hands, to what their fingers have made.

CONTINUED ON NEXT PAGE

15. For it is by grace you have been saved, through faith — and this not from yourselves, it is the gift of God.
16. But for those who are self-seeking and who reject the truth and follow evil, there will be wrath and anger.
17. But you, son of man, listen to what I say to you. Do not rebel like that rebellious house; open your mouth and eat what I give you. 
18. Look! My lover! Look! Here he comes, leaping across the mountains, bounding over the hills.
19. And may I have a letter to Asaph, keeper of the king's forest, so he will give me timber to make beams for the gates of the citadel by the temple and for the city wall and for the residence I will occupy?
20. Now the Lord God had planted a garden in the east, in Eden; and there he put the man he had formed.
21. If you really keep the royal law found in Scripture, "Love your neighbor as yourself," you are doing right.

GENESIS, EPHESIANS, EZEKIEL, ISAIAH, JAMES, JOB, 1 JOHN, JOSHUA, LUKE, MATTHEW, NEHEMIAH, ROMANS, RUTH, SONG OF SOLOMON

This is what God said about the angels: "God makes his angels become like winds. He makes his servants become like flames of fire." (HEBREWS 1:7)

Who did an angel speak these words to?

1. "Do not be afraid to take Mary home as your wife, because what is conceived in her is from the Holy Spirit" (**MATTHEW 1:20**).
2. "Get up and eat" (**1 KINGS 19:3-6**).
3. "Do not lay a hand on the boy." (**GENESIS 22:11-12**).
4. "Seal up what the seven thunders have said and do not write it down" (**REVELATION 10:4, 1:9**).
5. "Greetings, you who are highly favored! The Lord is with you" (**LUKE 1:28**).
6. "Now you will be silent and not able to speak until the day this happens, because you did not believe my words, which will come true at their proper time." (**LUKE 1:20**).

Don't know an ANSWER? Look first in the Bible, then in the back of this book...

Bible Commands

Loving God means obeying his commands.
And God's commands are not too hard for us. (1 JOHN 5:3)

In Matthew 22:34-40, a religious leader in Jerusalem asked Jesus this question: "Which is the greatest commandment in the Law?" Supply the missing words in His answer:

"'*(1)*________ the Lord your *(2)*______ with all your heart and with *(3)*____ your soul and with all *(4)*______ mind.' This is the first and greatest *(5)*________________. And the second is like it: 'Love your *(6)*__________ as yourself.' All the Law and the Prophets hang on these two commandments."

SCRIPTURE SCRAMBLE: Rearrange the words in each numbered sentence below so that these commands of Jesus read correctly.

7. *Give asks the who you, to one*
turn do and not away
borrow from who the wants one from to you.

MATTHEW 5:42

8. *first kingdom righteousness, Seek his and his*
things and all these
given you will to as well. be

MATTHEW 6:33

9. *give When the you to needy,*
left know your not do let hand
right doing. what your hand is

MATTHEW 6:3

10. *harvest The plentiful is*
workers but are the few.
harvest, Lord Ask the of the therefore,
workers field. to out into send his harvest

MATTHEW 9:37–38

Don't know an ANSWER? Look first in the Bible, then in the back of this book...

He was equal with God. But he did not think that being equal with God was something to be held on to.... He was born to be a man and became like a servant. (PHILIPPIANS 2:6-7)

WHAT DID JESUS SAY?—Answer "Jesus" for each of these statements in the gospels which Jesus said; answer "Someone Else" for each one which Jesus did not say:

1. "I am not the Christ but am sent ahead of him" (JOHN 3:28).
2. "My food is to do the will of him who sent me and to finish his work" (JOHN 4:34).
3. "I know that Messiah is coming. When he comes, he will explain everything to us" (JOHN 4:25).
4. "I have no one to help me get into the pool when the water is stirred. While I am trying to get in, someone else goes down ahead of me" (JOHN 5:7).

5. "I do nothing on my own, but speak just what the Father has taught me. The one who sent me is with me; he has not left me alone, for I always do what pleases him" (JOHN 8:28–29).
6. "I tell you the truth, if anyone keeps my word, he will never see death" (JOHN 8:51).
7. "You were steeped in sin at birth; how dare you lecture us!" (JOHN 9:34).
8. "The miracles I do in my Father's name speak for me" (JOHN 10:25).
9. "Why then do you accuse me of blasphemy because I said, 'I am God's Son'? Do not believe me unless I do what my Father does" (JOHN 10:36–37).
10. "You shall never wash my feet" (JOHN 13:8).
11. "You are right in saying I am a king. In fact, for this reason I was born, and for this I came into the world, to testify to the truth. Everyone who is on the side of truth listens to me" (JOHN 18:37).
12. "Whoever lives and believes in me will never die" (JOHN 11:26).
13. "Don't you realize I have power either to free you or to crucify you?" (JOHN 19:10).
14. "We have no king but Caesar" (JOHN 19:15).
15. "Peace be with you! As the Father has sent me, I am sending you" (JOHN 20:21).

Jesus Our Leader

*You call me "Teacher" and "Lord." And this is right, because that is what I am. (**Jesus,** in John 13:13)*

SCRIPTURE SCRAMBLE: Rearrange the words in each numbered sentence below so that the verses read correctly.

1. *food My to is do*
   will the of who me him sent
   finish work. to and his

   John 4:34

2. *will does the Whoever*
   heaven Father my of in
   brother sister mother. and is my and

   Matthew 12:50

3. In John 10:1-18, Jesus compares us to sheep. And He said, "I am the Good ______________."

▼ ▼ ▼

In Luke 15:1-7, Jesus tells the story about someone losing one of his 100 sheep.

4. What does this person do when he discovers he has lost one of his sheep?
5. What does he do with the lost sheep when he finds it?
6. What does he do when he gets the lost sheep home?

The righteous are as bold as a lion. (PROVERBS 28:1)

TRIPLE SEARCH:

How many words can you find that are included in ALL THREE of these verses?

Do not be afraid of what you are about to suffer. I tell you, the devil will put some of you in prison to test you. (REVELATION 2:10)

Do not be afraid, little flock, for your Father has been pleased to give you the kingdom. (LUKE 12:32)

In God, whose word I praise, in God I trust; I will not be afraid. (PSALM 56:4)

EXTRA EXERCISE—*Keep your Bible handy!*

STRONG STARTS — Name the book that begins with each of these verses:

1. That which was from the beginning, which we have heard, which we have seen with our eyes, which we have looked at and our hands have touched.
2. In the third year of the reign of Jehoiakim king of Judah, Nebuchadnezzar king of Babylon came to Jerusalem and besieged it. And the Lord delivered Jehoiakim king of Judah into his hand.
3. Solomon son of David established himself firmly over his kingdom, for the Lord his God was with him and made him exceedingly great.
4. In the past God spoke to our forefathers through the prophets at many times and in various ways, but in these last days he has spoken to us by his Son.
5. After Ahab's death, Moab rebelled against Israel.
6. In the first year of Cyrus king of Persia, in order to fulfill the word of the Lord spoken by Jeremiah, the Lord moved the heart of Cyrus king of Persia to make a proclamation throughout his realm and to put it in writing.

All Your Heart

Love the Lord your God with all your heart…
*(**Jesus,** in MATTHEW 22:37)*

UNLOCK THE TREASURE BOX:

What's the KEY WORD *(it goes where you see the* ***) in this passage?

______

* * *

(It begins with the letter "H")

"For in this *** we are saved. But *** that is seen is no *** at all. Who ***s for what he already has? But if we *** for what we do not yet have, we wait for it patiently."

— ROMANS 8:24-25

Love the Lord your God...with all your mind...
*(**Jesus,** in MATTHEW 22:37)*

SWORD-SHARPENERS—"The sword of the Spirit...is the word of God" (**EPHESIANS 6:17**). For each verse below, fill in the right word at the beginning — at the "tip of the sword." (When you read down, the first letters of these words will spell the word PEACE.)

"P_______ your hope in God" (**PSALM 42:5**).

"E_______ of us should please his neighbor, for his good" (**ROMANS 15:2**).

"A_______ your sons will be taught by the Lord, and great will be your children's peace" (**ISAIAH 54:13**).

"C_______ with me by yourselves to a quiet place and get some rest" (**MARK 6:31**).

"E_______ that hear and eyes that see — the Lord has made them both" (**PROVERBS 20:12**).

Jesus Our King

He is Lord of lords and King of kings—and with him will be his called, chosen and faithful followers. (*REVELATION 17:14*)

THE KING'S WORDS—Who did Jesus make each of these statements to?

1. "Freely you have received, freely give" (**MATTHEW 10:8**).
2. "Be careful. Be on your guard against the yeast of the Pharisees and Sadducees" (**MATTHEW 16:6**).
3. "The Son of Man must suffer many things and be rejected by the elders, chief priests, and teachers of the law, and he must be killed and on the third day be raised to life" (**LUKE 9:22**).
4. "It is written, 'My house will be called a house of prayer,' but you are making it a 'den of robbers'" (**MATTHEW 21:13**).

5. "Come down immediately. I must stay at your house today" (Luke 19:5).
6. "Let the little children come to me, and do not hinder them, for the kingdom of heaven belongs to such as these" (Matthew 19:14).
7. "It is not right to take the children's bread and toss it to their dogs" (Matthew 15:26).
8. "This very night you will all fall away on account of me" (Matthew 26:31).
9. "Get behind me, Satan! You are a stumbling block to me; you do not have in mind the things of God, but the things of men" (Matthew 16:23).
10. "You don't know what you are asking. Can you drink the cup I drink or be baptized with the baptism I am baptized with?" (Mark 10:38).
11. "May you never bear fruit again!" (Matthew 21:19).
12. "I tell you the truth, one of you will betray me" (Matthew 26:21).
13. "Why do you persecute me? It is hard to kick against the goads" (Acts 26:14-15).
14. "You are the ones who justify yourselves in the eyes of men, but God knows your hearts. What is highly valued among men is detestable in God's sight" (Luke 16:14-15).

God's People

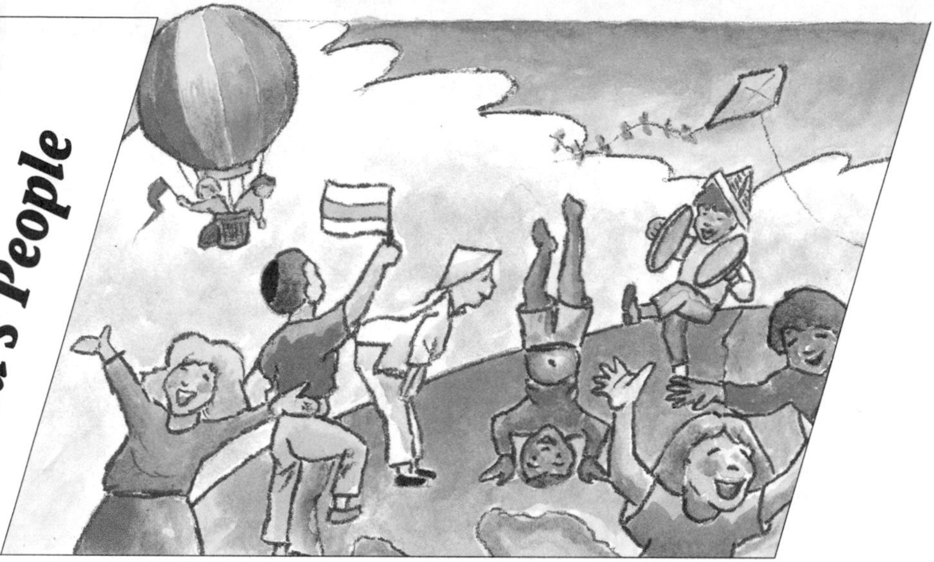

You are a chosen people, a royal priesthood, a holy nation, a people belonging to God. (1 Peter 2:9)

FAMILY MATCHUP: <u>FATHER AND DAUGHTER</u>—From this list of men, match each one with the name of his daughter in the numbered list below.

David Jacob Laban Bethuel Saul Job

1. Dinah (Genesis 34:1)
2. Jemimah, Keziah, and Keren (Job 42:14)
3. Merab and Michal (1 Samuel 18:17–20)
4. Rachel and Leah (Genesis 29:16)
5. Rebekah (Genesis 24:15)
6. Tamar (2 Samuel 13:1)

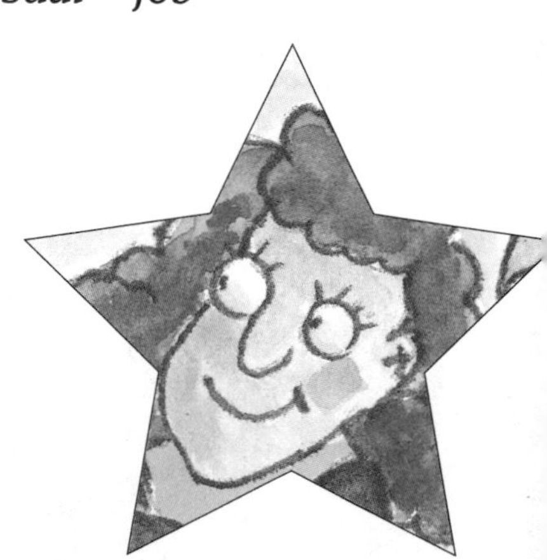

FAMILY MATCHUP: <u>MOTHER AND DAUGHTER</u>—Match each woman with the name of her daughter in the numbered list.

MOTHERS: Jochebed Leah

7. Miriam (NUMBERS 26:59)
8. Dinah (GENESIS 34:1)

FAMILY MATCHUP: <u>HUSBAND AND WIFE</u>—Match each man with the name of his wife in the numbered list.

Ahab Aquila David Elimelech Elkanah Herod the King Hosea Jacob Joseph (in Genesis) Lappidoth Moses Nabal Uriah

9. Asenath (GENESIS 41:50-52)
10. Deborah (JUDGES 4:4)
11. Gomer (HOSEA 1:1-3)
12. Hannah (1 SAMUEL 1)
13. Herodias (MARK 6:17-20)
14. Jezebel (1 KINGS 16:29-31)
15. Leah (GENESIS 29:16-32)
16. Michal (1 SAMUEL 18:20-29)
17. Naomi (RUTH 1:2)
18. Priscilla (ACTS 18:1-2)
19. Zipporah (EXODUS 2:16-22)
20. Abigail (first husband— 1 SAMUEL 25:3)
21. Abigail (second husband— 1 SAMUEL 25:35-42)
22. Bathsheba (first husband— 2 SAMUEL 11:3)
23. Bathsheba (second husband— 2 SAMUEL 11:26-27)

The Promised Land

Then the Lord said, "This is the land I promised on oath to Abraham, Isaac and Jacob." (Deuteronomy 34:4)

SCRIPTURE SCRAMBLE—In Deuteronomy 31:8, God spoke the following words to the people of Israel. He wanted to encourage them as they prepared to finally enter the land that had been promised to them long ago. Rearrange the words so that each line reads correctly.

1. *goes The himself you Lord before*
2. *you; be will with and*
3. *never you he leave will*
4. *forsake nor you.*
5. *not be Do. afraid;*
6. *be discouraged. not do*

WHICH WAY?—
If you were starting a trip from Jerusalem back in Bible times, which direction would you go to get to these places? Match each place name to an arrow on the map.

PLACES: *Mount Nebo* *Mount Sinai* *Assyria* *Ephesus* *Samaria* *Emmaus* *Edom*

1. ____________

2. ____________

3. ____________

JERUSALEM

7. ____________

4. ____________

6. ____________

5. ____________

N

Talking with God

Ask and it will be given to you; seek and you will find; knock and the door will be opened to you. (**Jesus,** in MATTHEW 7:7)

FAMOUS PRAYERS IN THE BIBLE—Tell who prayed each one of these prayers:

1. "Lord, you know everyone's heart. Show us which of these two men you have chosen to take over this apostolic ministry, which Judas left to go where he belongs" (ACTS 1:15–25).

2. "Ah, Sovereign Lord, you have made the heavens and the earth by your great power and outstretched arm. Nothing is too hard for you" (JEREMIAH 32:16-17).

3. "O Lord, turn Ahithophel's counsel into foolishness" (2 SAMUEL 15:31).

4. "Now, Lord, consider their threats and enable your servants to speak your word with great boldness. Stretch out your hand to heal and perform miraculous signs and wonders through the name of your holy servant Jesus" (ACTS 4:29-30).

5. "Give ear, O Lord, and hear; open your eyes, O Lord, and see; listen to all the words Sennacherib has sent to insult the living God" (ISAIAH 37:14-17).

6. "Now, O Lord, take away my life, for it is better for me to die than to live" (JONAH 4:3).

7. "Father, I want those you have given me to be with me where I am, and to see my glory, the glory you have given me because you loved me before the creation of the world" (JOHN 17:24).

8. "O Lord, I beg you, let the man of God you sent to us come again to teach us how to bring up the boy who is to be born" (JUDGES 13:8).

9. "You have given your servant this great victory. Must I now die of thirst and fall into the hands of the uncircumcised?" (JUDGES 15:18-19).

♥ What kinds of things do you think God would enjoy hearing now from *you*??

Don't know an ANSWER? Look first in the Bible, then in the back of this book...

The Way of Wisdom

Honey from the comb is sweet to your taste.
Know also that wisdom is sweet to your soul. (PROVERBS 24:13-14)

ABC's—Words that start with each letter of the alphabet will complete these verses from **PROVERBS,** the wisdom book. Use the clue that follows each letter to find the missing word.

A— *The help other people can give you when you need to decide what to do;* "Those who take a__________ are wise" **(13:10)**.

B— *To be brave and sure;* "The righteous are as b________ as a lion" **(28:1)**.

C— *To be told what you did wrong, and how you can do it right the next time;* "Anyone who loves learning accepts being c__________. But a person who hates being c__________ is stupid" **(12:1)**.

D— *Gives the training and teaching and correction that helps us live in the right way.* "The Lord d__________ those he loves, as a father d__________ the son he delights in" (3:12).

E— *A person who is always doing things AGAINST you;* "Don't be happy when your e______ is defeated. Don't be glad when he is overwhelmed" (24:17).

F— *A person who's always doing things FOR you;* "A f_______ loves you all the time" (17:17).

G— *Freely giving others what is yours;* "A g__________ person will be blessed because he shares his food with the poor" (22:9).

H— *Not being proud; not thinking too highly of yourself;* "H__________ comes before honor" (18:12).

I— *Honesty, sincerity, goodness;* "The man of i_________ walks securely, but he who takes crooked paths will be found out" (10:9).

J— *Fairness, rightness;* "Evil men do not understand j_________, but those who seek the Lord understand it fully" (28:5).

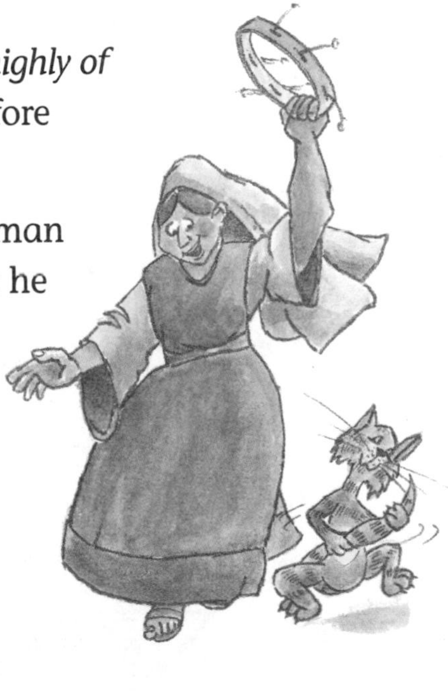

CONTINUED ON NEXT PAGE

K— *Being helpful to others;* "A k_____ person is doing himself a favor. But a cruel person brings trouble on himself" (11:17).

L— *Hearing and understanding;* "A person who answers without l________ is foolish and disgraceful" (18:13).

M—*Where your words come out;* "The m_______ of the righteous brings forth wisdom" (10:31).

N—*Someone who lives close to you;* "It is a sin to hate your n___________ " (14:21).

O—*To do what you're asked to do by someone who has authority over you;* "Don't make fun of your father. Don't refuse to o______ your mother" (30:17).

P— *Knowing how to wait quietly and gently;* "P_________ is better than strength. Controlling your temper is better than capturing a city" (16:32).

Q—*Unkind arguments that happen easily when you think too highly of yourself;* "Pride only breeds q__________" (13:10).

R—*Earned something good;* "The wise person is r__________ by his wisdom" (9:12).

S—*Something you know that most people don't know;* "A trust-worthy person can keep a s__________" (11:13).

T—*To believe and depend on;* "T_____ the Lord with all your heart. Don't depend on your own understanding" (3:5).

U—*To really know something;* "Then you will u__________ what is honest and fair and right. You will u__________ what is good to do" (2:9).

V—*The sound of someone speaking;* "Like a person, wisdom calls out to you. Understanding raises her v_______" (8:1).

W—*Doing your job;* "Those who w_____ hard make a profit. But those who only talk will be poor" (14:23).

X—*To bring greatness and honor;* "Righteousness ex________ a nation. But sin is a disgrace to any people" (14:34).

Y—*The time from one birthday to your next one;* "Through wisdom your days will be many, and y____ will be added to your life" (9:11).

Z—*Excited and eager;* "Always be z________ for the fear of the Lord" (23:17).

Don't know an ANSWER? Look first in the Bible, then in the back of this book...

*"The Holy Spirit...will teach you all things and will remind you of everything I have said to you." (**Jesus,** in John 14:26)*

What are the nine qualities or virtues which are called "the fruit of the Spirit," and found in Galatians 5:22-23? Say them in order:

1. L________ 2. J________ 3. P________

4. P________ 5. K________ 6. G________

7. F________ 8. G________ 9. S______-C________

♥ Perhaps one of these qualities is one that you especially need a lot more of in your life right now. If so, which one is it? In prayer, ask God now to give you more of this quality, through His Holy Spirit's presence in your life.

Love never fails. (1 CORINTHIANS 13:8)

SWORD-SHARPENERS—"The sword of the Spirit…is the word of God" (**EPHESIANS 6:17**). For each verse below, fill in the right word at the beginning — at the "tip of the sword." (When you read down, the first letters of these words will spell the word GOD.)

"G_______ is the Lord, and most worthy of praise" (**PSALM 48:1**).

"O_______ thing I ask of the Lord, this is what I seek: that I may dwell in the house of the Lord all the days of my life" (**PSALM 27:4**).

"D_______ and night they never stop saying: 'Holy, holy, holy is the Lord God Almighty, who was, and is, and is to come'" (**REVELATION 4:8**).

Don't know an ANSWER? Look first in the Bible, then in the back of this book…

What Happened When?

And God said, "Let there be lights in the expanse of the sky to separate the day from the night, and let them serve as signs to mark seasons and days and years." (Genesis 1:14)

TIME LINE: Match the following events with the approximate date shown beside the time line on the next page.

1. Paul's nephew tells Roman soldiers that the Jews in Jerusalem are planning to kill Paul. (Acts 23:12-22)
2. David sins against God by sinning against Uriah and his wife Bathsheba. (2 Samuel 11-12, Psalm 51)
3. Judah suggests to his brothers that they sell their younger brother Joseph as a slave. (Genesis 37:26-27)

4. Moses sends twelve spies into Canaan. Only Caleb and Joshua come back unafraid. (NUMBERS 13—14)

5. King Josiah weeps and tears his robe when he hears someone read from a scroll of the Scriptures that was found in the Temple. (2 CHRONICLES 34:14-33)

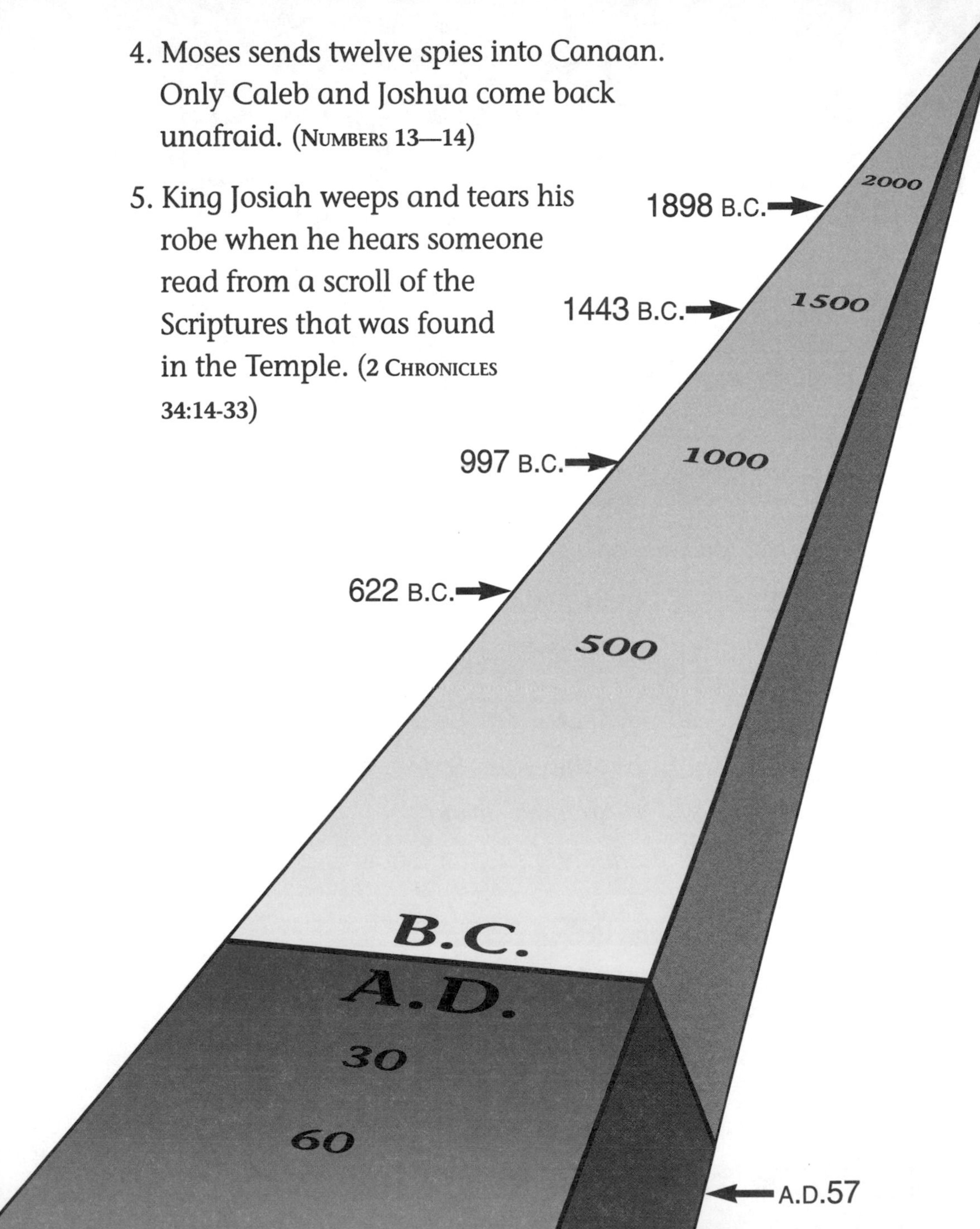

Jesus Our Savior

Jesus lives forever.... He is always able to save those who come to God through him. (HEBREWS 7:24-25)

SCRIPTURE SCRAMBLE: Rearrange the words in each numbered sentence below so that the verses read correctly.

1. *me, Whoever in believes*
   said, as the has Scripture
   water streams living of
   will from him. within flow

   JOHN 7:38

2. *doctor, is It healthy not the need who a*
   sick. but the

   MATTHEW 9:12

REPUTATION—What people in the Bible were known by these words?

1. "Sons of thunder" (Mark 3:17).
2. "Israel's singer of songs" (2 Samuel 23:1).
3. "That fox" (Luke 13:31-32).
4. "A lion's cub" (Genesis 49:9).
5. "A liar, and the father of lies" (John 8:44-45).
6. "Son of Encouragement" (Acts 4:36).
7. "God's friend" (James 2:23).
8. "A wild donkey of a man" (Genesis 16:11-12).
9. "A man after God's own heart" (Acts 13:22).
10. "Father of many nations" (Genesis 17:4-5).
11. "A mighty prince among us" (Genesis 23:6).
12. "Jerub-baal" (Judges 6:32).
13. "Troubler of Israel" (1 Kings 18:17-18).
14. "A prince among his brothers" (Genesis 49:26).
15. "A rawboned donkey lying down between two saddlebags" (Genesis 49:14).
16. "A doe set free" (Genesis 49:21).
17. "A serpent by the roadside, a viper along the path" (Genesis 49:17).
18. "A ravenous wolf" (Genesis 49:27).
19. "The Son of the Most High" (Luke 1:32).

Praise be to the Lord my Rock, who trains my hands for war, my fingers for battle. (PSALM 144:1)

WHOSE ARMY?

1. When Zedekiah was king of Judah, whose army captured Jerusalem and burned it, and took most of the people away as prisoners? (2 KINGS 25)
2. Whose army was destroyed in the Red Sea when they tried to go after the people of Israel? (EXODUS 14:23-28)
3. One day, as Joshua and the people of Israel drew near to Jericho and prepared to take it, Joshua looked up and saw a man standing in front of him with a drawn sword in his hand. Joshua asked him, "Are you for us or for our enemies?" The man answered that he was the commander of someone's army. Whose army was it? (JOSHUA 5:13-15)

“ ”

FAMOUS ANSWERS

Tell who made each of these answers to the questions that were asked them in the Scriptures:

1. “The woman you put here with me—she gave me some fruit from the tree, and I ate it.” (Genesis 3:12).
2. “I don’t know. Am I my brother’s keeper?” (Genesis 4:9).
3. “You are the Christ, the Son of the living God” (Matthew 16:16).
4. “I tell you, not seven times, but seventy-seven times” (Matthew 18:22).
5. “I have told you already and you did not listen. Why do you want to hear it again? Do you want to become his disciples, too?” (John 9:27).
6. “No, I insist on paying you for it. I will not sacrifice to the Lord my God burnt offerings that cost me nothing” (2 Samuel 24:24).
7. “I merely tasted a little honey with the end of my staff. And now must I die?” (1 Samuel 14:43).
8. “Lord, to whom shall we go? You have the words of eternal life. We believe and know that you are the Holy One of God” (John 6:68-69).
9. “I am the voice of one calling in the desert, ‘Make straight the way for the Lord’” (John 1:23).

Coming Kingdom

I will not drink of this fruit of the vine again until that day when I drink it new with you in my Father's kingdom. (***Jesus,*** *in* MATTHEW *26:29)*

In Matthew 13:47-50, Jesus said the kingdom of heaven is like a net that fishermen let down into a lake, catching all kinds of fish. The net was full of both good fish and bad fish. Then the fishermen pulled the net on shore.

1. What did they do with the good fish?
2. What did they do with the bad fish?
3. Jesus said the bad fish are like wicked people. What did He say will happen to them?

I remind you to fan into flame the gift of God which is in you.
(2 Timothy 1:6)

SWORD-SHARPENERS—"The sword of the Spirit...is the word of God" (**Ephesians 6:17**). For each verse below, fill in the right word at the beginning — at the "tip of the sword." (When you read down, the first letters of these words will spell the word HOLY.)

"H_______ is not here; he has risen, just as he said" (**Matthew 28:6**).

"O_______ more I will shake not only the earth but also the heavens" (**Hebrews 12:26**).

"L_______ everything that has breath praise the Lord" (**Psalm 150:6**).

"Y_______ after year this man went up from his town to worship and sacrifice to the Lord Almighty at Shiloh" (**1 Samuel 1:3**).

Don't know an ANSWER? Look first in the Bible, then in the back of this book...

The Great Battle

Our fight is not against people on earth.... We are fighting against the spiritual powers of evil in the heavenly world. (EPHESIANS 6:12)

To be strong in the Lord's power, we are told in Ephesians 6:10-18 to "put on the full armor of God, so that when the day of evil comes, you may be able to stand your ground."

Match these words below with the parts of armor on the next page, according to the teaching in Ephesians 6:14-17.

truth	*righteousness*
gospel of peace	*faith*
salvation	*the Spirit*

1. the helmet of

____

2. the sword of

____ __________,
which is the
Word of God

3. the shield of

___________,
with which you
can extinguish
all the flaming
arrows of the
evil one

4. the breast-
plate of

____

5. the belt of

____
buckled around
your waist

6. your feet
fitted with the
readiness that
comes from the

____

___ __________

Treasure Chest

Store up for yourselves treasures in heaven, where moth and rust do not destroy, and where thieves do not break in and steal.
(***Jesus,*** *in* MATTHEW *6:20*)

UNLOCK THE TREASURE BOX:

What's the KEY WORD *(it goes where you see the ****) in this passage?

____

* * *

(It begins with the letter "N")

"The *** man makes *** plans, and by *** deeds he stands." — **ISAIAH 32:8**

"The seed on good soil stands for those with a *** and good heart, who hear the word, retain it, and by persevering produce a crop." — Jesus, in **LUKE 8:15**

WHO SAID THIS?

Tell who spoke each of these statements or questions in Scripture:

1. "How long will you waver between two opinions? If the Lord is God, follow him; but if Baal is God, follow him" (1 Kings 18:21).
2. "Was it because there were no graves in Egypt that you brought us to the desert to die? What have you done to us by bringing us out of Egypt? Didn't we say to you in Egypt, 'Leave us alone; let us serve the Egyptians'? It would have been better for us to serve the Egyptians than to die in the desert!" (Exodus 14:10-12).
3. "Do you understand what I have done for you?" (John 13:12).
4. "Give to Caesar what is Caesar's, and to God what is God's" (Matthew 22:21).
5. "The Lord has torn the kingdom of Israel from you today and has given it to one of your neighbors—to one better than you. He who is the Glory of Israel does not lie or change his mind; for he is not a man, that he should change his mind" (1 Samuel 15:28-29).
6. "I consider my life worth nothing to me, if only I may finish the race and complete the task the Lord Jesus has given me—the task of testifying to the gospel of God's grace" (Acts 20:24).

5

Faces and Places

The Sovereign Lord will wipe away the tears from all faces.
(Isaiah 25:8)

REPUTATION: Who does the Bible say these things about?

1. "The Lord was with _____ as he grew up, and he let none of his words fall to the ground" (**1 Samuel 3:19**).
2. "Now _____ was a very humble man, more humble than anyone else on the face of the earth" (**Numbers 12:3**).
3. "God gave _____ wisdom and very great insight.... He was wiser than any other man" (**1 Kings 4:29-31**).
4. "_____ trusted in the Lord, the God of Israel. There was no one like him among all the kings of Judah, either before him or after him" (**2 Kings 18:5**).

♥ What's *your* reputation? What does God think of *you?*

E-Z EASY: The names of each of these Bible characters includes both the letters "E" and "Z". Can you give each name?

5. She was a relative of Mary (Jesus' mother), and Mary went to visit her before Jesus was born. (Luke 1:36-42)
6. This king had a dream about an enormous statue. Only Daniel could explain the dream to him. (Daniel 2)
7. This queen was one of the most evil women in the Bible. When she died, dogs ate her body. (1 Kings 18:4, 2 Kings 9:30–37)
8. He was the father of John the Baptist. When he did not believe the angel who told him he was to have a son, he became unable to speak. *(His name is sometimes spelled with an "A" instead of an "E".)* (Luke 1:13-22)
9. This king wept and prayed when he became ill, so God gave him another fifteen years to live. As a sign to this man, God made the sun's shadow go back ten steps on a stairway. (Isaiah 38:1-8)
10. These three men all have Old Testament books named after them. One was a prophet, one was a priest, and the other was both a prophet and a priest.

11 This man watched his two brothers burn to death when they did not show respect for God's holiness. He later became Israel's second high priest after his father Aaron died. (Leviticus 10:12, Numbers 20:22–29)

Don't know an ANSWER? Look first in the Bible, then in the back of this book...

Jesus Our Friend

I have called you friends, for everything that I learned from my Father I have made known to you. (***Jesus***, *in* JOHN *15:15*)

SCRIPTURE SCRAMBLE: Rearrange the words in each numbered sentence below so that the verses read correctly.

1. *three together two or in come name, my Where them. there I with am*

   MATTHEW 18:20

2. *did Whatever you for one brothers mine, of the of least these of did you me. for*

   MATTHEW 25:40

♥ What have *you* done recently to help someone else?

3. *you; leave Peace I with*
give peace my I you.
world I do as not to you the gives. give
troubled, Do your let not hearts be
afraid. and not be do

JOHN 14:27

4. *am! Here I*
knock. stand I at door the and
voice If hears anyone my
opens door, and the
eat I will come and in him, with
me. with and he

REVELATION 3:20

5. *Spirit, God is*
must worship worshipers and his
truth. spirit in in and

JOHN 4:24

6. *man believes a in me, When*
only, me believe he does not in
but one in who sent the me.

JOHN 12:44

7. *joined What God together, has*
separate. not man let

MATTHEW 19:6

They were brave warriors, ready for battle... Their faces were the faces of lions...they were as swift as gazelles in the mountains. (1 CHRONICLES 12:8)

WHICH HAPPENED FIRST?

1. David killed Goliath, or David was anointed king by Samuel? (1 SAMUEL 16—17)
2. Paul was arrested, or Paul was shipwrecked? (ACTS 21, 27)
3. Joseph was put in jail, or Joseph became a great leader in Egypt? (GENESIS 39—41)

▼ ▼ ▼

4. This great preacher received instruction about Jesus from Priscilla and Aquila. In Scripture he is called "a learned man, with a thorough knowledge of the Scriptures." Who was he? (ACTS 18:24-28)

WHAT ARE THEY HOLDING? There's something different in the hands of each of these Bible characters. What is it?

5. When Moses throws it to the ground, it will turn into a snake. (EXODUS 4:2-4, 7:8-9)
6. David will use this to kill Goliath. (1 SAMUEL 17:38-40)
7. In John's dream recorded in the book of Revelation, he sees seven of these in Jesus' right hand. (REVELATION 1:16)
8. As Gideon's men attack the Midianites, they each hold a torch in their left hand, and this in their right. (JUDGES 7:19–21)
9. Jesus takes this, breaks it, and gives it to His disciples as He says, "This is my body." (MARK 14:22)
10. The workers under Nehemiah who are rebuilding Jerusalem's walls have their tools and materials in one hand, and this in the other. (NEHEMIAH 4:16-18)
11. Miriam takes this and leads the women of Israel in a song and dance, for Pharaoh's chariots and horsemen have been destroyed in the sea. (EXODUS 15:19-21)
12. After David has killed Goliath, he's holding this when Israel's army commanders bring him before King Saul. (1 SAMUEL 17:57)

♥ Who is your favorite hero in the Bible? Why is he or she your favorite?

Don't know an ANSWER? Look first in the Bible, then in the back of this book...

FAMOUS QUESTIONS

WHO ASKED THIS?—Tell who asked each one of these questions in the Bible:

1. "Where is your brother Abel?" (Genesis 4:9).
2. "Why couldn't we drive it out?" (Matthew 17:19).
3. "Will you sweep away the righteous with the wicked? What if there are fifty righteous people in the city? Will you really sweep it away and not spare the place for the sake of the fifty righteous people in it?" (Genesis 18:23-24).
4. "By what authority are you doing these things? And who gave you this authority?" (Matthew 21:23).
5. "Whose portrait is this? And whose inscription?" (Matthew 22:20).
6. "We have left everything to follow you. What then will there be for us?" (Matthew 19:27).
7. "How can I be sure of this? I am an old man and my wife is well along in years" (Luke 1:18).
8. "Hannah, why are you weeping? Why don't you eat? Why are you downhearted? Don't I mean more to you than ten sons?" (1 Samuel 1:8).
9. "What then is this bleating of sheep in my ears? What is this lowing of cattle that I hear?" (1 Samuel 15:14).

The Lord is faithful to all his promises. (PSALM 145:13)

PROMISE POWER—Match the right ending *(from the list below)* to each of these powerful promises in God's Word.

1. Blessed is the man who perseveres under trial, because when he has stood the test...
2. God has given us eternal life, and this life is in his Son....
3. Everything is possible...

(A)• *for him who believes* (MARK 9:23).

(B)• *he will receive the crown of life that God has promised to those who love him* (JAMES 1:12).

(C)• *he who has the Son has life; he who does not have the Son of God does not have life* (1 JOHN 5:11-12).

Don't know an ANSWER? Look first in the Bible, then in the back of this book...

I will remember the deeds of the Lord; yes, I will remember your miracles of long ago. (PSALM 77:11)

THE PLAGUES UPON EGYPT—From the results listed here, identify each of the plagues upon Egypt after Moses and Aaron asked Pharaoh to let the Hebrew people go.

1. This made fish die, the river smelled awful, and people were without water. It started when Moses struck his staff on the River Nile. What was it that happened? (EXODUS 7:14-24)
2. The land was completely covered with these slimy creatures, and they were in people's houses and even in their beds. They started coming when Aaron stretched out his hands. What were they? (EXODUS 8:1-15)
3. Aaron stretched out his staff and touched the dust. The dust turned into these tiny insects, and they went after both people and animals. What were they? (EXODUS 8:16-19)

4. More insects! This kind came in dense swarms, pouring into Pharaoh's palace and the houses of the Egyptians; but there were none of them in the houses of the Israelites. What kind of insects were they? (Exodus 8:20–32)
5. This brought death to particular kinds of useful animals belonging to the Egyptians. But the same kinds of animals belonging to the Israelites were not killed. What kinds of animals were struck by this plague? (Exodus 9:1–7)
6. Next came a certain kind of sore that broke out on the skin of all the Egyptians. It started when Moses took handfuls of soot from a furnace and threw it into the air. What were these sores? (Exodus 9:8–12)
7. This plague was a big change in the weather. It killed anyone who was outside in it, and it started when Moses stretched his hand toward the sky. But it didn't touch the places where the Israelites lived. What was it? (Exodus 9:13–35)
8. Moses stretched out his staff, and a steady east wind brought a third kind of insects. They totally covered the ground, destroying any crops and trees still left after the seventh plague. What were these insects? (Exodus 10:1–20)
9. For three days, no one could see in Egypt—except for the Israelites. What happened in this plague? (Exodus 10:21–29)
10. The last plague was the worst. Again the Israelites were spared, in what became known as the Passover. What did God do to Egypt in this final plague? (Exodus 11:1—12:33)

Don't know an ANSWER? Look first in the Bible, then in the back of this book...

Knowing God

We will not fear even if the oceans roar and foam, or if the mountains shake at the raging sea.... God says, "Be quiet and know that I am God." (PSALM 46:3-10)

FRIENDS OF GOD:

1. This great man of faith in the Old Testament "was called God's friend." Who was he? (JAMES 2:23, 2 CHRONICLES 20:7)
2. Doctor Luke wrote the gospel of Luke and the book of Acts to this man, whose name means "friend of God." What was his name? (LUKE 1:1-4, ACTS 1:1)
3. In James 4:4 we are told that if we choose to be a "friend of the world," we become whose enemy?

WHICH BOOK?—Tell which book of the Bible each of these verses about God's character is from:

4. For God did not send his Son into the world to condemn the world, but to save the world through him. (JAMES, JOHN, OR EXODUS?)
5. Then Israel said to Joseph, "I am about to die, but God will be with you and take you back to the land of your fathers." (JUDGES, 2 CHRONICLES, OR GENESIS?)
6. For to us a child is born, to us a son is given, and the government will be on his shoulders. And he will be called Wonderful Counselor, Mighty God, Everlasting Father, Prince of Peace. (RUTH, ROMANS, OR ISAIAH?)
7. And Moses recited the words of this song from beginning to end in the hearing of the whole assembly of Israel: "...I will proclaim the name of the Lord. Oh, praise the greatness of our God! He is the Rock, his works are perfect, and all his ways are just. A faithful God who does no wrong, upright and just is he." (DEUTERONOMY, JUDGES, OR EZEKIEL?)
8. For our God is a consuming fire. (HEBREWS, 1 JOHN, OR RUTH?)
9. Know that the Lord is God. It is he who made us, and we are his; we are his people, the sheep of his pasture. (ESTHER, PSALMS, OR JAMES?)
10. Then Hannah prayed and said: "My heart rejoices in the Lord; in the Lord my horn is lifted high...There is no one holy like the Lord; there is no one besides you; there is no Rock like our God. (1 SAMUEL, NUMBERS, OR ISAIAH?)

Don't know an ANSWER? Look first in the Bible, then in the back of this book...

Born Again

I tell you the truth, no one can see the kingdom of God unless he is born again. (**Jesus**, *in* JOHN *3:3*)

UNLOCK THE TREASURE BOX:

What's the KEY WORD *(it goes where you see the* ***) in this passage?

____

* * *

(It begins with the letter "J")

"Our mouths were filled with laughter, our tongues with songs of ***.... The Lord has done great things for us, and we are filled with ***.... Those who sow in tears will reap with songs of ***. He who goes out weeping, carrying seed to sow, will return with songs of ***."

— PSALM 126:2-6

DREAMS IN THE BIBLE

Who had each of these dreams?

1. A boy and his older brothers are binding sheaves of grain out in the field, when suddenly the boy's sheaf rises and stands upright, while his brothers' sheaves bow down to it. (GENESIS 37:5-7)
2. Out of the Nile river came seven fat, sleek cows, grazing among the reeds. Then came seven ugly and lean cows, and they ate up the fat cows. But the lean cows still looked as skinny as ever. (GENESIS 41:17-21)
3. A round loaf of barley bread comes crashing into the Midianite camp and overturns a tent. (JUDGES 7:13)
4. A man is standing and begging, "Come over to Macedonia and help us." (ACTS 16:9)
5. A stairway reaches from earth to heaven, with angels on it, and the Lord is standing above it. (GENESIS 28:12-13)
6. A statue appears with a gold head, silver chest and arms, bronze belly and thighs, iron legs, and clay feet. (DANIEL 2:31–33)
7. The Lord appears, and says, "Ask me for whatever you want me to give you." (1 KINGS 3:5)
8. The Lord appears, and says, "Get up, take the child and his mother and escape to Egypt. Stay there until I tell you, for Herod is going to search for the child to kill him." (MATTHEW 2:13)

The name of the Lord is a strong tower; the righteous run to it and are safe. (PROVERBS 18:10)

WORDS OF DUTY —Tell who made each of these statements in the Scriptures:

1. "No servant can serve two masters. Either he will hate the one and love the other, or he will be devoted to the one and despise the other. You cannot serve both God and Money" (LUKE 16:13).

2. "Do not be afraid. Stand firm and you will see the deliverance the Lord will bring you today. The Egyptians you see today you will never see again. The Lord will fight for you; you need only to be still" (EXODUS 14:13-14).

“ ”

THE VOICE OF GOD

Each of these statements was spoken in the Scriptures by God. For each one, tell who God was speaking to.

1. “I anointed you king over Israel, and I delivered you from the hand of Saul.... I gave you the house of Israel and Judah. And if all this had been too little, I would have given you even more. Why did you despise the word of the Lord by doing what is evil in his eyes?.... Now, therefore, the sword will never depart from your house, because you despised me and took the wife of Uriah the Hittite to be your own” (2 Samuel 12:7-10).
2. “Listen to all that the people are saying to you; it is not you they have rejected, but they have rejected me as their king.... Now listen to them; but warn them solemnly and let them know what the king who will reign over them will do” (1 Samuel 8:7-9).
3. “In the place where dogs licked up Naboth’s blood, dogs will lick up your blood—yes, yours!” (1 Kings 21:19).
4. “Yet I reserve seven thousand in Israel — all whose knees have not bowed down to Baal and all whose mouths have not kissed him” (1 Kings 19:18).
5. “Do not be afraid; keep on speaking, do not be silent. For I am with you, and no one is going to attack and harm you, because I have many people in this city” (Acts 18:9–10).

Bible Numbers

How precious to me are your thoughts, O God!
How vast is the sum of them! Were I to count them,
they would outnumber the grains of sand. (PSALM 139:17-18)

1. Only twelve of the 66 books in the Bible have a name that does not refer to a person or a group of people. What are these twelve books?

2. Eighteen of the 66 books in the Bible have a number or numbers in their name. What are these eighteen books?

3. What book of the Bible has the shortest name?

4. Which books of the Bible have the most letters in their name?

5. Many of the books of the Bible have long names, but there are more books with only four letters in their name than any other number of letters. Can you name all twelve of the books with four-letter names?

Some were laughed at and beaten. Others were tied and put into prison. They were killed with stones and they were cut in half. (HEBREWS 11:36-37)

SWORD-SHARPENERS—"The sword of the Spirit...is the word of God" (**EPHESIANS 6:17**). For each verse below, fill in the right word at the beginning — at the "tip of the sword." (When you read down, the first letters of these words will spell the word BRAVE.)

"B_______ still and know that I am God; I will be exalted among the nations, I will be exalted in the earth" (**PSALM 46:10**).

"R_______ in me, and I will remain in you" (**JOHN 15:4**).

"A_______ me when I call to you, O my righteous God. Give me relief from my distress" (**PSALM 4:1**).

"V_______ soon my anger against you will end" (**ISAIAH 10:25**).

"E_______ is possible for him who believes" (**MARK 9:23**).

Children in the Bible

Children are a gift from the Lord. (PSALM 127:3)

1. This boy was the second one born to his mother and father, but the first son became sick and died shortly after he was born. The Lord loved the second boy, and sent word through the prophet Nathan to call him Jedidiah, which means "loved by the Lord." He is much better known, however, by another name the Lord gave him, a name which means "peace." When he grew up, he became one of Israel's greatest and most famous kings. Who was he?
   (2 SAMUEL 12:24–25, 1 CHRONICLES 22:6–10)

2. A verse about this boy's childhood says that he "grew and became strong in spirit" (LUKE 1:80). He was a cousin to Jesus, and later a "forerunner" to Jesus. Who was he?

★ GOLD STAR SPECIAL ★

CAREFUL CLOSINGS — Name the book that ends with each of these verses:

1. I charge you before the Lord to have this letter read to all the brothers. The grace of our Lord Jesus Christ be with you.
2. Who is wise? He will realize these things. Who is discerning? He will understand them. The ways of the Lord are right; the righteous walk in them, but the rebellious stumble in them.
3. Remember this: Whoever turns a sinner from the error of his way will save him from death and cover over a multitude of sins.
4. For God will bring every deed into judgment, including every hidden thing, whether it is good or evil.
5. Charm is deceptive, and beauty is fleeting; but a woman who fears the Lord is to be praised. Give her the reward she has earned, and let her works bring her praise at the city gate.
6. Let everything that has breath praise the Lord. Praise the Lord.
7. I, Paul, write this greeting in my own hand. Remember my chains. Grace be with you.
8. Grace to all who love our Lord Jesus Christ with an undying love.

Women in the Bible

Many women do noble things.... A woman who respects the Lord should be praised. (*PROVERBS 31:29-30*)

1. Naomi's friends were talking to her about Ruth, and called her "your daughter-in-law, who loves you and who is better to you than seven ________." (**RUTH 4:15**)
2. Who is the first woman mentioned in the "Hall of Faith" in Hebrews 11? (**HEBREWS 11:11**)
3. Besides Mary, His mother, what four other women are named in the family tree of Jesus, as recorded in Matthew 1:1-16?
4. Along with her husband, she risked her life for Paul. Who was she? (**ROMANS 16:3-4**)
5. She and the prophet Nathan together carried out a plan to ensure that her son became Israel's next king. (**1 KINGS 1:11–30**)

WORDS FROM WIVES TO THEIR HUSBANDS—We don't know the names of the women who said the things below to their husbands, but we do know who their husbands were. Name each husband whose wife told him…

6. to curse God and die. (Job 2:9)
7. to not have anything to do with condemning Jesus, because she'd had a bad dream about Him. (Matthew 27:19)
8. that Joseph the Hebrew "came to me to make sport of me." (Genesis 39)

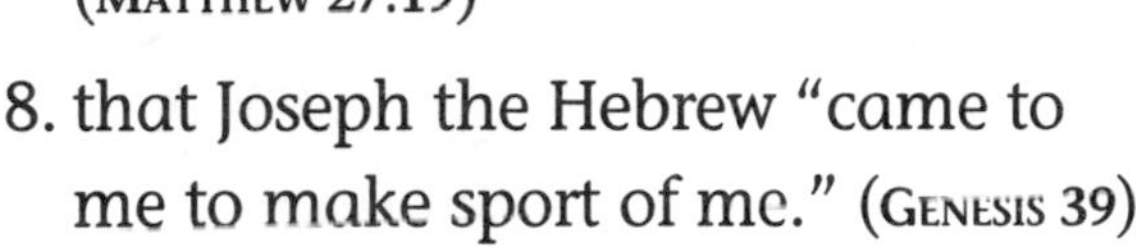

9. that her servant girl told her about a prophet in Israel who could heal his leprosy. (2 Kings 5:1-4)

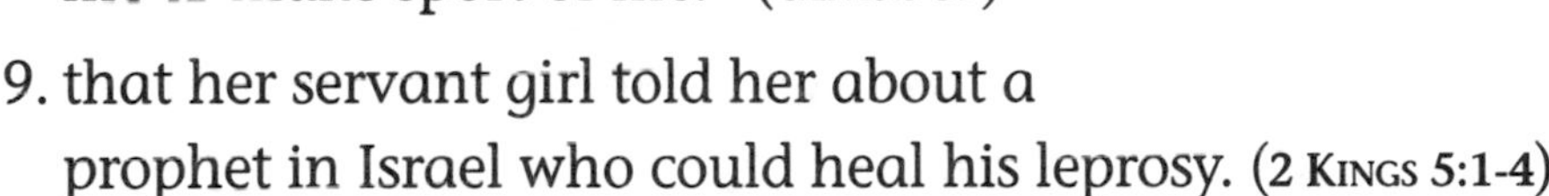

10. that she had met a man of God who looked like an angel, who told her that she would have a son, and who said that the boy would be set apart for God. (Judges 13:1-7)

▼▼▼

11. This man's wife looked back upon Sodom and Gomorrah after God told them not to, and she turned into a pillar of salt. Who was her husband? (Genesis 19:17-26)
12. This king of Israel had a son who was ill. He asked his wife to disguise herself, and to go and ask the prophet Ahijah if the boy was going to die.Who was this king? (1 Kings 14:1-19)

You should recognize the value of men like these.
(1 Corinthians 16:18)

DISCIPLE DRILL: For the following questions, each answer is the name of one or more of the twelve men who made up Jesus' team of disciples. (Some names are used more than once.)

1. Jesus once told him, "Satan has asked to sift you as wheat. But I have prayed for you, that your faith may not fail. And when you have turned back, strengthen your brothers." (Luke 22:31–32)
2. Jesus saw this man standing under a fig tree. And He said, "Here is a true Israelite, in whom there is nothing false." (John 1:47)
3. This disciple said to Jesus, "We have left everything to follow you!" (Matthew 19:27)

4. In the gospel he wrote, this disciple calls himself “the disciple whom Jesus loved.” (13:23, 19:26, 20:2, 21:7)
5. Simon Peter once asked a question about this disciple, but Jesus answered, “If I want him to remain alive until I return, what is that to you? You must follow me.” (John 21:20-22)
6. From the cross, Jesus saw his mother standing next to this disciple. And He said to him, “Here is your mother.” From that time on, this disciple took care of Jesus’ mother. (John 19:25–27)
7. This disciple was praying on his roof, and had a vision in which he saw something like a large sheet being let down to earth from heaven, with animals on it. (Acts 12:1-19)
8. After Jesus had gone back to heaven, King Herod put this disciple to death with the sword. (Acts 12:2)
9. This disciple is known to us by two names, one beginning with “B” and one with “N”. (Matthew 10:3, John 21:2)
10. This disciple is also known to us by two names, one beginning with “M” and one with “L”. (Luke 5:27-28, Matthew 9:9-13)
11. This disciple was called “the Zealot.” (Luke 6:15)
12. This disciple, whose father’s name was James, is known to us by two names. One begins with “J” and one with “T”. (The “J” name is in Luke 6:16, the “T” name is in Matthew 10:3.)
13. This disciple’s mother-in-law was healed by Jesus. (Mark 1:30–31)

CONTINUED ON NEXT PAGE

14. Jesus called these two disciples "Boanerges," which means, "Sons of Thunder." (MARK 3:17)
15. Jesus once told this disciple, "When you are old you will stretch out your hands, and someone else will dress you and lead you where you do not want to go." (JOHN 21:18)
16. When Jesus told this man how He recognized him, the man said, "Rabbi, you are the Son of God; you are the King of Israel." Jesus answered, "You believe because I told you I saw you under the fig tree. You shall see greater things than that. I tell you the truth, you shall see heaven open, and the angels of God ascending and descending on the Son of Man." (JOHN 1:47-51)
17. When Jesus said, "If you really knew me, you would know my Father as well," this disciple said, "Lord, show us the Father, and that will be enough for us." Then Jesus said, "Don't you know me, even after I have been among you such a long time? Anyone who has seen me has seen the Father." Who was this disciple? (JOHN 14:7–9)
18. In John 1:35-39, two disciples heard John the Baptist say about Jesus, "Behold the Lamb of God!" These two disciples followed Jesus, and asked Him where He was staying. He answered, "Come, and you will see." So they went and spent the day with Jesus. One of these two disciples is unnamed, but we know the name of the other. Who was he?

19. When Jesus said, "You know the way to the place where I am going," this disciple said to Him, "Lord, we don't know where you are going, so how can we know the way?" Jesus answered, "I am the way and the truth and the life." Who was this disciple? (John 14:4–6)

20. When Jesus said, "Where I am going you cannot follow now, but you will follow later," this disciple said, "Lord, why can't I follow you now? I will lay down my life for you." Who was this disciple? (John 13:36–38)

21. When Mary of Bethany poured expensive perfume on the feet of Jesus, this disciple said, "Why wasn't this perfume sold and the money given to the poor?" But he said this because he was a thief, and used to steal from the money the disciples kept. (John 12:1-6)

22. When Jesus wanted to feed a huge crowd of hungry people, and there seemed to be no food, this disciple said, "Here is a boy with five small barley loaves and two small fish, but how far will they go among so many?" (John 6:8)

23. A crippled beggar sitting in front of the Temple in Jerusalem asked these two disciples for money. But they gave him something better: In the name of Jesus, they healed him so he could walk. Which two of the disciples did this? (Acts 3)

24. This disciple was led by the Holy Spirit to visit the home of Cornelius, a Roman centurion. (Acts 10)

CONTINUED ON NEXT PAGE

25. Jesus once said to this fisherman, "Put out into deep water, and let down the nets for a catch." And the fisherman answered, "Master, we've worked hard all night and haven't caught anything. But because You say so, I will let down the nets." Who was this man? (LUKE 5:4-5)

26. After Jesus had risen from the dead, many of the disciples went fishing. Then they saw Jesus on the shore. One of the disciples put on his cloak and jumped into the water and swam to Him, while the others brought the boat in, filled with fish. Who was the disciple who jumped in? (JOHN 21:7-8)

27. These two disciples were thrown in jail in Jerusalem, because they were teaching people about Jesus. They were brought before the Temple leaders, and commanded not to speak or teach in the name of Jesus. They answered, "Judge for yourselves whether it is right in God's sight to obey you rather than God. For we cannot help speaking about what we have seen and heard." Who were these two men? (ACTS 4)

28. This disciple said to Jesus, "Master, we saw a man driving out demons in your name and we tried to stop him, because he is not one of us." But Jesus said, "Do not stop him, for whoever is not against you is for you." Who was this disciple? (LUKE 9:49-50)

29. Jesus sent these two disciples ahead of Him to make preparations for the Passover meal which they ate together the night before He was killed. (LUKE 22:7-13)

30. These two disciples came with their mother to Jesus with a special request: In the future kingdom of glory, they wanted to sit next to Jesus, one on the right of Him and one on the left. (MATTHEW 20:20-28, MARK 10:35-45)

31. This disciple was from the town of Cana in Galilee, where Jesus turned water into wine. (JOHN 21:2)

32. In Jerusalem, these two disciples went to tell Jesus about some Greeks who wanted to see Him. (JOHN 12:20-22)

33. After Jesus had risen from the dead, He said to this doubting disciple, "Put your finger here; see my hands. Reach out your hand and put it into my side. Stop doubting and believe." (JOHN 20:24-29)

34. This disciple went to the chief priests and asked, "What are you willing to give me if I hand Jesus over to you?" And they gave him thirty silver coins. (MATTHEW 26:14-16)

35. These two disciples were fishermen with their father Zebedee. (MATTHEW 4:21-22)

36. After one of the disciples betrayed Jesus and then killed himself, a new man was chosen to be part of the Twelve. Who was this new disciple? (ACTS 1:12-26)

Our Home in Heaven

Our homeland is in heaven, and we are waiting for our Savior,
the Lord Jesus Christ, to come from heaven. (PHILIPPIANS 3:20)

SCRIPTURE SCRAMBLE: Rearrange the words in each numbered sentence below so that the verses read correctly.

1. *angels And he send his will*
trumpet loud a with call,
gather and his they elect will
winds, the four from
end heavens from one of the
other. to the

MATTHEW 24:31

2. *ready, must You also be*
come Son because the of Man will
hour expect at an when you not him. do

MATTHEW 24:44

“ ”

WHO SAID THIS?

Tell who spoke each of these statements or questions in Scripture:

1. “I’m disgusted with living because of these Hittite women. If Jacob takes a wife from among the women of this land, from Hittite women like these, my life will not be worth living” (Genesis 27:46).
2. “Do you see this woman? I came into your house. You did not give me any water for my feet, but she wet my feet with her tears and wiped them with her hair. You did not give me a kiss, but this woman, from the time I entered, has not stopped kissing my feet. You did not put oil on my head, but she has poured perfume on my feet” (Luke 7:44–46).
3. “But Lord, by this time there is a bad odor, for he has been there four days” (John 11:39).
4. “This child is destined to cause the falling and rising of many in Israel, and to be a sign that will be spoken against, so that the thoughts of many hearts will be revealed. And a sword will pierce your own soul too” (Luke 2:34-35).
5. “Let me go through your flocks today and remove from them every speckled or spotted sheep, every dark-colored lamb and every spotted or speckled goat. They will be my wages” (Genesis 30:32).

Book, Chapter & Verse

These words are like nails that have been driven in firmly. They are wise teachings that come from God the Shepherd. (ECCLESIASTES 12:11)

CAN YOU FIND IT?

1. What's the longest chapter in the Bible, and how many verses does it have?
2. What's the shortest chapter in the Bible, and how many verses does it have?
3. What's the only verse in the Bible that contains all three of these words: *God, loved,* and *world?*
4. What's the longest book in the Bible?

Angels

This is what God said about the angels: "God makes his angels become like winds. He makes his servants become like flames of fire." (HEBREWS 1:7)

Who did an angel speak these words to?

1. "Look up and see that all the male goats mating with the flock are streaked, speckled or spotted, for I have seen all that Laban has been doing to you" (**GENESIS 31:10-13**).
2. "Go back to your mistress and submit to her. I will so increase your descendants that they will be too numerous to count" (**GENESIS 16:7-10**).
3. "Son of man, understand that the vision concerns the time of the end" (**DANIEL 8:15-17**).
4. "These words are trustworthy and true. The Lord, the God of the spirits of the prophets, sent his angel to show his servants the things that must soon take place" (**REVELATION 22:6,8**).

Don't know an ANSWER? Look first in the Bible, then in the back of this book...

Bible Commands

Loving God means obeying his commands.
And God's commands are not too hard for us. (1 JOHN 5:3)

UNLOCK THE TREASURE BOX:

What's the KEY WORD *(it goes where you see the* ***) in this passage?

____

* * *

(It begins with the letter "L")

"A new command I give you: *** one another. As I have ***d you, so you must *** one another. By this all men will know that you are my disciples, if you *** one another."

— JOHN 13:34-35

BIG TEN: Complete the missing words in each numbered sentence below so that the Ten Commandments (EXODUS 20) read correctly.

I am the Lord your God, who brought you out of Egypt, out of the land of slavery.

1. *You shall have no other* _____ __________ _____.

2. *You shall not make for yourself* ___ _____...

3. *You shall not misuse* ____ ______ ___ ____ ______ ______ ______...

4. *Remember* ____ ____________ _____ *by keeping it holy.*

5. *Honor* _____ _________ ____ _____ _________...

6. *You shall not* _______.

7. *You shall not* _______ ________.

8. *You shall not* ______.

9. *You shall not* _____ _______ ___________ ______ _____ _________.

10. *You shall not* _______...

Don't know an ANSWER? Look first in the Bible, then in the back of this book...

He was equal with God. But he did not think that being equal with God was something to be held on to.... He was born to be a man and became like a servant. (PHILIPPIANS 2:6-7)

POWER PASSAGE: Philippians 2:5-11

JESUS CHRIST

Our Example of How Not to Be Selfish

On the following page, add the right words in the right places to complete this inspiring passage. Choose them from the list of words here:

bring Christ Father gave God

death everyone humbled knee Lord

man name nothing raised think

In your lives you must (1)______ and act like (2)______ Jesus.

Christ himself was like (3)______ in everything.

He was equal with God.

But he did not think that being equal with God

was something to be held on to.

He (4)______ up his place with God

and made himself (5)______.

He was born to be a man

and became like a servant.

And when he was living as a (6)______

he (7)______ himself and was fully obedient to God.

He obeyed even when that caused his (8)______

— death on a cross.

So God (9)______ Christ to the highest place.

God made the (10)______ of Christ

greater than every other name.

God wants every (11)______ to bow to Jesus—

(12)______ in heaven, on earth, and under the earth.

Everyone will say, "Jesus Christ is (13)______"

and (14)______ glory to God the (15)______.

Don't know an ANSWER? Look first in the Bible, then in the back of this book...

Jesus Our Leader

You call me "Teacher" and "Lord." And this is right, because that is what I am. (***Jesus,*** *in* JOHN *13:13)*

SCRIPTURE SCRAMBLE: Rearrange the words in each numbered sentence below so that the verses read correctly.

1. *Now Teacher, I, your Lord and that*
   washed have feet, your
   wash feet. also one should you another's

   JOHN 13:14

2. *example I an have you set*
   done that you do as I should for have you.

   JOHN 13:15

3. *know Now that these you things,*
   do be blessed if you them. you will

   JOHN 13:17

EXTRA EXERCISE—***Keep your Bible handy!***

LAST LOOKS IN THE BOOKS — Name the Bible book that ends with each of these verses:

1. In those days Israel had no king; everyone did as he saw fit.
2. So the cloud of the Lord was over the tabernacle by day, and fire was in the cloud by night, in the sight of all the house of Israel during all their travels.
3. So Joseph died at the age of a hundred and ten. And after they embalmed him, he was placed in a coffin in Egypt.
4. Come away, my lover, and be like a gazelle, or like a young stag on the spice-laden mountains.
5. The Sovereign Lord is my strength; he makes my feet like the feet of a deer, he enables me to go on the heights.
6. For no one has ever shown the mighty power or performed the awesome deeds that Moses did in the sight of all Israel.
7. While he was blessing them, he left them and was taken up into heaven. Then they worshiped him and returned to Jerusalem with great joy. And they stayed continually at the temple, praising God.

Bold and Brave

The righteous are as bold as a lion. (Proverbs 28:1)

1. What woman of Israel drove a tent peg into the head of Sisera, the Canaanite king? (Judges 4:17-22)
2. Who killed a thousand Philistines with the jawbone of a donkey? (Judges 15:15-16)
3. Who went down into a pit on a snowy day and killed a lion, and also struck down an Egyptian who was seven and a half feet tall? (1 Chronicles 11:22-23)
4. This nephew of David struck down eighteen thousand Edomites in the Valley of Salt, and also killed three hundred men with a spear. Who was he? (1 Chronicles 18:12, 11:20, 2:13–16)

WHO SAID THIS?

Tell who made each of these statements in the Scriptures:

1. "Why do you just keep looking at each other? I have heard that there is grain in Egypt. Go down there and buy some for us, so that we may live and not die" (Genesis 42:1–2).
2. "Put into deep water, and let down the nets for a catch" (Luke 5:4).
3. "The report I heard in my own country about your achievements and your wisdom is true.... Indeed, not even half was told me; in wisdom and wealth you have far exceeded the report I heard" (1 Kings 10:6-7).
4. "Go, make the tomb as secure as you know how" (Matthew 27:65).
5. "I tell you the truth, before Abraham was born, I am!" (John 8:58).
6. "If they do not listen to Moses and the Prophets, they will not be convinced even if someone rises from the dead" (Luke 16:31).
7. "The days of mourning for my father are near; then I will kill my brother Jacob" (Genesis 27:41).
8. "Your name will no longer be Jacob, but Israel, because you have struggled with God and with men and have overcome" (Genesis 32:28).

Love the Lord your God with all your heart...
*(**Jesus,** in MATTHEW 22:37)*

UNLOCK THE TREASURE BOX:

What's the KEY WORD *(it goes where you see the ***)* in this passage?

____

* * *

(It begins with the letter "P")

Pray for the *** of Jerusalem: "May those who love you be secure. May there be *** within your walls and security within your citadels." For the sake of my brothers and friends, I will say, "*** be within you."

— PSALM 122:6-8

Love the Lord your God…with all your mind…
*(**Jesus,** in MATTHEW 22:37)*

SWORD-SHARPENERS—"The sword of the Spirit…is the word of God" (EPHESIANS 6:17). For each verse below, fill in the right word at the beginning — at the "tip of the sword." (When you read down, the first letters of these words will spell the word THINK.)

"T_______ me your way, O Lord, and I will walk in your truth" (PSALM 86:11).

"H_______ the word of the Lord, O nations" (JEREMIAH 31:10).

"I_______ anyone thinks he is something when he is nothing, he deceives himself" (GALATIANS 6:3).

"N_______ be lacking in zeal, but keep your spiritual fervor, serving the Lord" (ROMANS 12:11).

"K_______ their thoughts, Jesus said, 'Why do you entertain evil thoughts in your hearts?'" (MATTHEW 9:4).

Don't know an ANSWER? Look first in the Bible, then in the back of this book…

Jesus Our King

He is Lord of lords and King of kings—and with him will be his called, chosen and faithful followers. (REVELATION 17:14)

WHO DID JESUS make each of these statements to?

1. "What you are about to do, do quickly" (JOHN 13:27).
2. "I am willing. Be clean!" (MATTHEW 8:3).
3. "They do not need to go away. You give them something to eat" (MATTHEW 14:16).
4. "Put your finger here; see my hands. Reach out your hand and put it into my side. Stop doubting and believe" (JOHN 20:27).
5. "Watch and pray so that you will not fall into temptation. The spirit is willing, but the body is weak" (MATTHEW 26:41).

SCRIPTURE SCRAMBLE: Rearrange the words on each line to find out what Jesus said about Himself in the book of Revelation:

6. *Alpha I the the Omega, am and*
First the Last, and the
Beginning End. the and the

REVELATION 22:13

7. *Root I am the*
David, and the of Offspring
Star. bright and the Morning

REVELATION 22:16

8. *Omega, I am Alpha the and the*
who and who is, was,
who and come, is to
Almighty. the

REVELATION 1:8

9. *Living I am One; the*
dead, I was
alive behold ever! and I am ever for and
keys hold and I the
death and Hades. of

REVELATION 1:18

You are a chosen people, a royal priesthood, a holy nation, a people belonging to God. (1 Peter 2:9)

FAMILY MATCHUP: <u>MOTHER AND SON</u>—From this list of women, match each one with the name of her son in the numbered list below.

MOTHERS: Eunice Hagar Jochebed Leah Naomi Rachel Rahab

1. Aaron and Moses (**Exodus 6:20**)
2. Boaz (**Matthew 1:5**)
3. Ishmael (**Genesis 16**)
4. Joseph and Benjamin (**Genesis 46:19**)
5. Mahlon and Kilion (**Ruth 1:2**)
6. Reuben, Simeon, Levi, Judah, Issachar, Zebulun (**Genesis 35:23**)
7. Timothy (**2 Timothy 1:5**)

FAMILY MATCHUP: FATHER AND SON—From this list of men, match each one with the name of his son in the numbered list below.

FATHERS: Amoz Amram Boaz Buzi David Eli Elkanah Gideon (Jerub-baal) Haran Hilkiah Jonathan Joseph (in Genesis) Kish Lamech Lot Manoah Obed Nun Solomon Terah

8. Abimelech (Judges 8:28-31)
9. Abraham or Abram (Genesis 11:27)
10. Ezekiel (Ezekiel 1:3)
11. Hophni and Phinehas (1 Samuel 1:3)
12. Isaiah (Isaiah 1:1)
13. Jeremiah (Jeremiah 1:1)
14. Jesse (Ruth 4:17)
15. Joshua (Numbers 27:18)
16. Lot (Genesis 11:27)
17. Mephibosheth (2 Samuel 4:4)
18. Moab and Ben-Ammi (Genesis 19:36-38)
19. Manasseh and Ephraim (Genesis 41:50-52)
20. Moses (Exodus 6:20)
21. Noah (Genesis 5:28-29)
22. Obed (Ruth 4:17)
23. Rehoboam (1 Kings 11:43)
24. Samson (Judges 13)
25. Samuel (1 Samuel 1)
26. Saul (1 Samuel 9:1-2)
27. Solomon, Amnon, Absalom (1 Kings 2, 1 Chronicles 3:1-9)

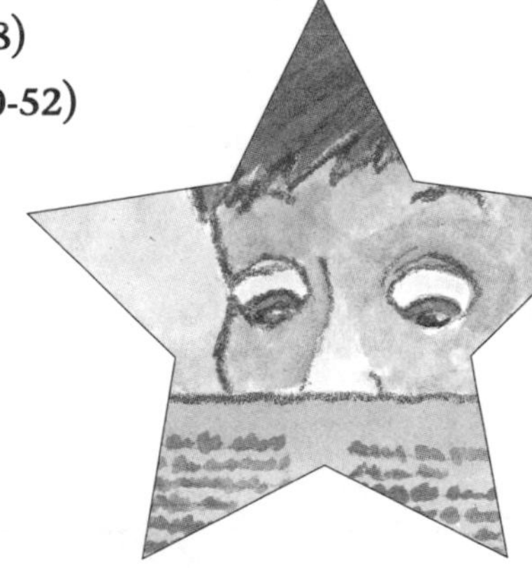

Don't know an ANSWER? Look first in the Bible, then in the back of this book...

The Promised Land

Then the Lord said, "This is the land I promised on oath to Abraham, Isaac and Jacob." (DEUTERONOMY 34:4)

WHO SAID THESE THINGS about the Promised Land?

1. "We went into the land to which you sent us, and it does flow with milk and honey! Here is its fruit. But the people who live there are powerful, and the cities are fortified and very large. We even saw descendants of Anak there." (**NUMBERS 13:26-29**).

2. "Not one of you will enter the land I swore with uplifted hand to make your home, except Caleb son of Jephunneh and Joshua son of Nun" (**NUMBERS 14:30**).

♥ What keeps us sometimes from receiving and enjoying what God has promised us?

WHICH WAY?—

If you were starting a trip from Jerusalem back in Bible times, which direction would you go to get to these places? Match each place name to an arrow on the map.

PLACES: *Shiloh* *Ashdod* *Gilgal* *Ziklag* *Joppa* *Tekoa* *Heshbon* *Hebron*

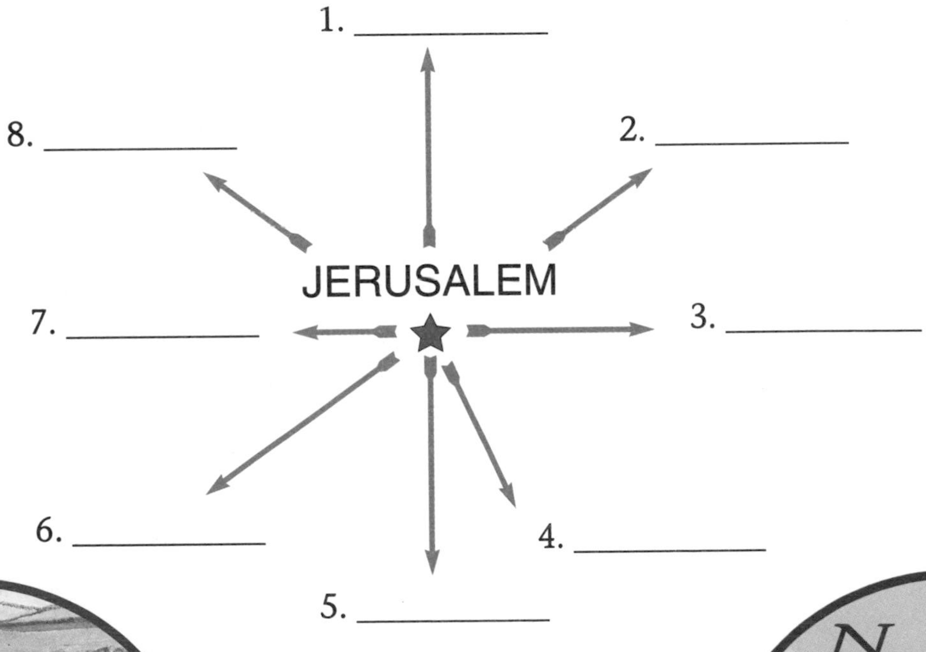

1. ____________

8. ____________

2. ____________

JERUSALEM

7. ____________

3. ____________

6. ____________

4. ____________

5. ____________

N

*Ask and it will be given to you; seek and you will find; knock and the door will be opened to you. (**Jesus,** in Matthew 7:7)*

FAMOUS PRAYERS IN THE BIBLE—Tell who prayed each one of these prayers:

1. Ah, Sovereign Lord, why did you ever bring this people across the Jordan to deliver us into the hands of the Amorites to destroy us? If only we had been content to stay on the other side of the Jordan! O Lord, what can I say, now that Israel has been routed by its enemies? The Canaanites and the other people of the country will hear about this and they will surround us and wipe out our name from the earth. What then will you do for your own great name?" (Joshua 7:6–9).

2. "God, I thank you that I am not like other men — robbers, evildoers, adulterers — or even like this tax collector. I fast twice a week and give a tenth of all I get" (LUKE 18:11-12).

3. "God, have mercy on me, a sinner" (LUKE 18:13).

4. "O Lord, listen! O Lord, forgive! O Lord, hear and act! For your sake, O my God, do not delay, because your city and your people bear your Name" (DANIEL 9:19).

5. "Remember Tobiah and Sanballat, O my God, because of what they have done; remember also the prophetess Noadiah and the rest of the prophets who have been trying to intimidate me" (NEHEMIAH 6:14).

6. "But will God really dwell on earth? The heavens, even the highest heaven, cannot contain you. How much less this temple I have built! Yet give attention to your servant's prayer and his plea for mercy, O Lord my God.... May your eyes be open toward this temple night and day" (1 KINGS 8:22–30).

7. "Oh, that you would bless me and enlarge my territory! Let your hand be with me, and keep me from harm so that I will be free from pain" (1 CHRONICLES 4:9-10).

8. "Remember, O Lord, how I have walked before you faithfully and with wholehearted devotion and have done what is good in your eyes" (ISAIAH 38:2-3).

Honey from the comb is sweet to your taste.
Know also that wisdom is sweet to your soul. (PROVERBS 24:13-14)

ABC's—Words that start with each letter of the alphabet will complete these verses from **PROVERBS**, the wisdom book. Use the clue that follows each letter to find the missing word.

A— *Not subtract;* "Let the wise listen and a_____ to their learning, and let the discerning get guidance" (1:5).

B— *Torn, destroyed;* "Like a city whose walls are b________ down is a man who lacks self-control" (25:28).

C— *Speak, ask;* "My son, if you accept my words and store up my commands within you, turning your ear to wisdom and applying your heart to understanding, and if you c_____ out for insight and cry aloud for understanding, and if you look for it as for silver and search for it as for hidden treasure, then you will understand the fear of the Lord and find the knowledge of God" (2:1–5).

D— *Save, rescue;* "Do not say, 'I'll pay you back for this wrong!' Wait for the Lord, and he will d__________ you" (20:22).

E— *In all places;* "The eyes of the Lord are e___________, keeping watch on the wicked and the good" (15:3).

F— *A long distance away;* "The Lord is f________ from the wicked but he hears the prayer of the righteous" (15:29).

G— *The Lord;* "Let love and faithfulness never leave you; bind them around your neck, write them on the tablet of your heart. Then you will win favor and a good name in the sight of G______ and man" (3:3–4).

H— *A place to live;* "The wise woman builds her h________, but with her own hands the foolish one tears hers down" (14:1).

I— *Teaching;* "Listen to advice and accept i___________, and in the end you will be wise" (19:20).

CONTINUED ON NEXT PAGE

J— *Be a part of, take part with;* "Do not j______ those who drink too much wine or gorge themselves on meat" (23:20).

K— *A touch of the lips;* "An honest answer is like a k______ on the lips" (24:26).

L— *Cares for, nourishes, cherishes;* "The Lord detests the way of the wicked but he l______ those who pursue righteousness" (15:9).

M—*Why you do what you do;* "All a man's ways seem innocent to him, but m__________ are weighed by the Lord" (16:2).

N— *Where a bird lives;* "Like a bird that strays from its n______ is a man who strays from his home" (27:8).

O—*Not indoors;* "Finish your o_________ work and get your fields ready; after that, build your house" (24:27).

P— *A trail, a way to walk;* "The p______ of the righteous is like the first gleam of dawn, shining ever brighter till the full light of day" (4:18).

Q—*Hot-tempered;* "As charcoal to embers and as wood to fire, so is a q___________ man for kindling strife" (26:21).

R— *Scarce, not common;* "By wisdom a house is built, and through understanding it is established; through knowledge its rooms are filled with r_________ and beautiful treasures" (24:3–4).

S— *Be successful;* "There is no wisdom, no insight, no plan that can s__________ against the Lord" (21:30).

T— *Danger, misfortune;* "The righteous man is rescued from t_________, and it comes on the wicked instead" (11:8).

U— *Righteous, honest, good;* "The Lord detests the sacrifice of the wicked, but the prayer of the u_________ pleases him" (15:8).

V— *Winning;* "The Lord gives wisdom, and from his mouth come knowledge and understanding. He holds v___________ in store for the upright; he is a shield to those whose walk is blameless" (2:6–7).

W—*Measures; examines;* "All a man's ways seem right to him, but the Lord w_________ the heart" (21:2).

X— *Prepared, stirred together;* "Wisdom has built her house; she has hewn out its seven pillars. She has prepared her meat and __xed her wine; she has also set her table" (9:1–2).

Y— *Gives, provides;* "Blessed is the man who finds wisdom, the man who gains understanding, for she is more profitable than silver and y_______ better returns than gold" (3:13–14).

Z— *Excitement;* "It is not good to have z______ without knowledge, nor to be hasty and miss the way" (19:2).

Don't know an ANSWER? Look first in the Bible, then in the back of this book...

Holy Spirit

*"The Holy Spirit...will teach you all things and will remind you of everything I have said to you." (**Jesus,** in JOHN 14:26)*

Who said these things about the Holy Spirit in the book of Acts?

1. "Fellow Jews and all of you who live in Jerusalem, let me explain this to you; listen carefully to what I say. These men are not drunk, as you suppose. It's only nine in the morning! No, this is what was spoken by the prophet Joel: 'In the last days, God says, I will pour out my Spirit on all people'" (ACTS 2:14-17).
2. "Ananias, how is it that Satan has so filled your heart that you have lied to the Holy Spirit and have kept back for yourself some of the money you received for the land?" (ACTS 5:3).
3. "Can anyone keep these people from being baptized with water? They have received the Holy Spirit just as we have" (ACTS 10:47).

Love never fails. (1 Corinthians 13:8)

WORDS OF LOVE — Who spoke these words?

1. "The Lord bless you, my daughter. This kindness is greater than that which you showed earlier: You have not run after the younger men, whether rich or poor. And now, my daughter, don't be afraid. I will do for you all you ask" (**Ruth 3:10-11**).
2. "He must become greater; I must become less" (**John 3:30**).
3. "I grieve for you, Jonathan my brother; you were very dear to me. Your love for me was wonderful, more wonderful than that of women. How the mighty have fallen!" (**2 Samuel 1:26-27**)

What Happened When?

And God said, "Let there be lights in the expanse of the sky to separate the day from the night, and let them serve as signs to mark seasons and days and years." (GENESIS 1:14)

TIME LINE: Match the following events with the approximate date shown beside the time line on the next page.

1. The walls of Jericho come crashing down. (JOSHUA 6)
2. Daniel has a vision that begins with four great beasts coming out of a stormy sea. (DANIEL 7)
3. As the Jews hurl rocks at him, Stephen looks up and sees Jesus in heaven. (ACTS 7)

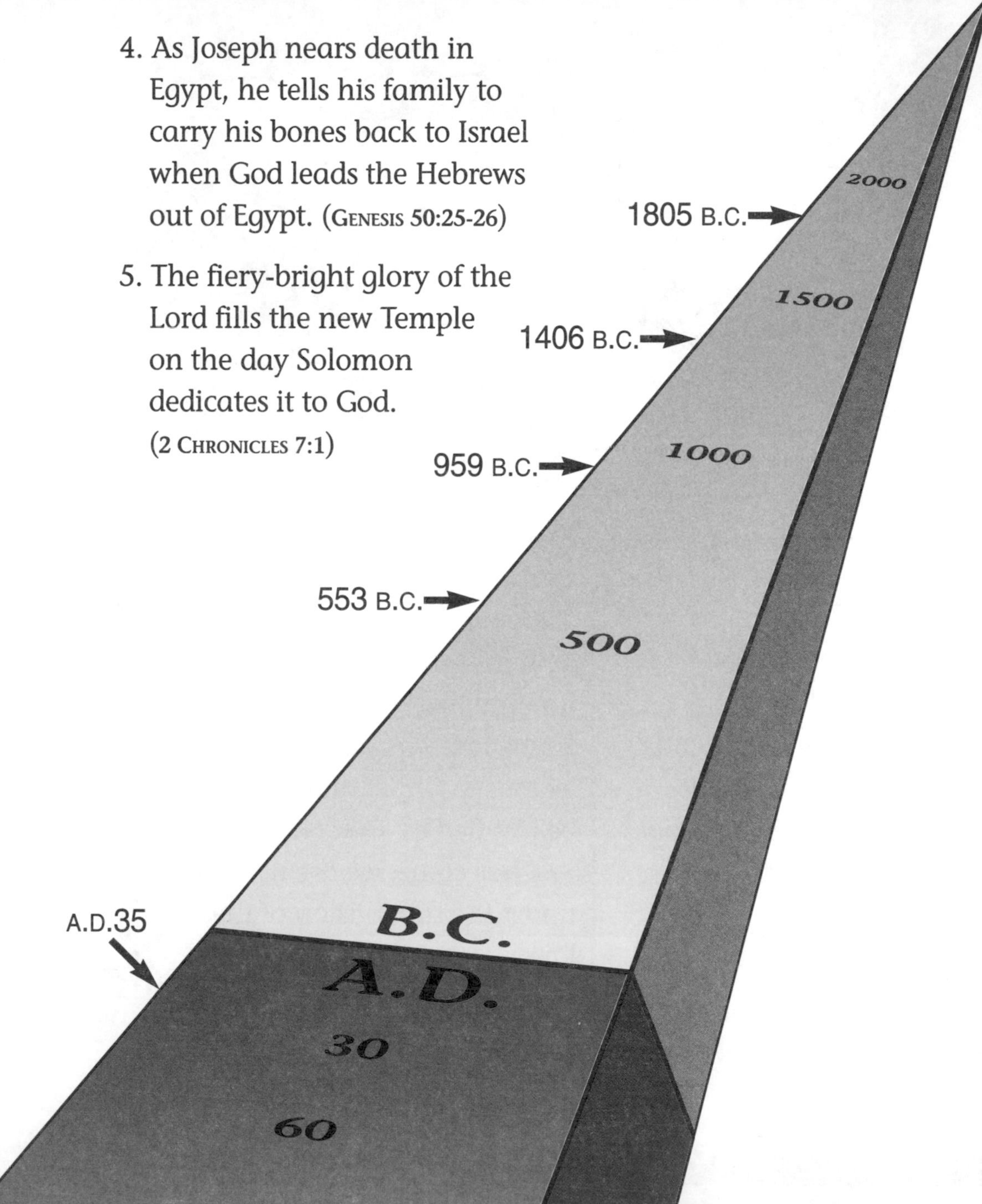

4. As Joseph nears death in Egypt, he tells his family to carry his bones back to Israel when God leads the Hebrews out of Egypt. (Genesis 50:25-26)
5. The fiery-bright glory of the Lord fills the new Temple on the day Solomon dedicates it to God. (2 Chronicles 7:1)
2000
1805 B.C.
1500
1406 B.C.
1000
959 B.C.
553 B.C.
500
A.D.35
B.C.
A.D.
30
60

Jesus Our Savior

Jesus lives forever.... He is always able to save those who come to God through him. (Hebrews 7:24-25)

UNLOCK THE TREASURE BOX:

What's the KEY WORD *(it goes where you see the* ***) in this passage?

____

* * *

(It begins with the letter "F")

"Before this *** came, we were held prisoners by the law, locked up until *** should be revealed. So the law was put in charge to lead us to Christ that we might be justified by ***. Now that *** has come, we are no longer under the supervision of the law."

— Galatians 3:23-25

THE MASTER'S WORDS—Who did Jesus make each of these statements to?

1. "We are going up to Jerusalem, and the Son of Man will be betrayed to the chief priests and the teachers of the law. They will condemn him to death and will turn him over to the Gentiles to be mocked and flogged and crucified. On the third day he will be raised to life!" (MATTHEW 20:18-19).
2. "Take heart, daughter, your faith has healed you" (MATTHEW 9:22).
3. "You are worried and upset about many things, but only one thing is needed. Mary has chosen what is better, and it will not be taken away from her" (LUKE 10:41-42).
4. "How often I have longed to gather your children together, as a hen gathers her chicks under her wings, but you were not willing" (MATTHEW 23:37).
5. "I tell you the truth, this very night, before the rooster crows, you will disown me three times" (MATTHEW 26:34).
6. "My soul is overwhelmed with sorrow to the point of death. Stay here and keep watch with me" (MATTHEW 26:38).
7. "Dear woman, here is your son" (JOHN 19:26).
8. "Here is your mother" (JOHN 19:27).
9. "Because you have seen me, you have believed; blessed are those who have not seen and yet have believed" (JOHN 20:29).

Don't know an ANSWER? Look first in the Bible, then in the back of this book...

Praise be to the Lord my Rock, who trains my hands for war, my fingers for battle. (PSALM 144:1)

THE WORDS OF SOLDIERS AND KINGS — Who made each of these statements in the Bible:

1. "No one ever spoke the way this man does" (JOHN 7:46).
2. "Hail, king of the Jews!" (MATTHEW 27:29).
3. "Surely he was the Son of God!" (MATTHEW 27:54).
4. "Do you speak Greek? Aren't you the Egyptian who started a revolt and led four thousand terrorists out into the desert some time ago?" (ACTS 21:37-38).
5. "I hereby put you in charge of the whole land of Egypt" (GENESIS 41:41).

6. "Saul and Jonathan — in life they were loved and gracious, and in death they were not parted. They were swifter than eagles, they were stronger than lions" (2 Samuel 1:23).

7. "With a donkey's jawbone I have made donkeys of them. With a donkey's jawbone I have killed a thousand men" (Judges 15:16).

8. "This day I defy the ranks of Israel! Give me a man and let us fight each other" (1 Samuel 17:10).

9. "Be strong, and let us fight bravely for our people and the cities of our God. The Lord will do what is good in his sight" (2 Samuel 10:12).

10. "Today you have humiliated all your men, who have just saved your life and the lives of your sons and daughters and the lives of your wives and concubines. You love those who hate you and hate those who love you. You have made it clear today that the commanders and their men mean nothing to you. I see that you would be pleased if Absalom were alive today and all of us were dead" (2 Samuel 19:5-6).

11. "Lord, I do not deserve to have you come under my roof. But just say the word, and my servant will be healed. For I myself am a man under authority, with soldiers under me. I tell this one, 'Go,' and he goes, and that one, 'Come,' and he comes. I say to my servant, 'Do this,' and he does it" (Matthew 8:8-9).

Coming Kingdom

I will not drink of this fruit of the vine again until that day when I drink it new with you in my Father's kingdom. (***Jesus,*** *in* MATTHEW *26:29)*

SCRIPTURE SCRAMBLE: Rearrange the words so that these "kingdom sayings" of Jesus read correctly.

1. *will nation, against Nation rise kingdom and kingdom. against*

   MATTHEW 24:7

2. *stands end He who to firm the be saved. will*

   MATTHEW 24:13

3. *see Son They will of the Man sky, clouds coming the of the on power great with glory. and*

   MATTHEW 24:30

I remind you to fan into flame the gift of God which is in you.
(2 Timothy 1:6)

SWORD-SHARPENERS—"The sword of the Spirit…is the word of God" (Ephesians 6:17). For each verse below, fill in the right word at the beginning — at the "tip of the sword." (When you read down, the first letters of these words will spell the word FIRE.)

"F_______, if you are willing, take this cup from me; yet not my will, but yours be done" (Luke 22:42).

"'I_______ not my word like fire,' declares the Lord, 'and like a hammer that breaks a rock in pieces?'" (Jeremiah 23:29).

"R_______ up and help us; redeem us because of your unfailing love" (Psalm 44:26).

"E_______ word of God is flawless; he is a shield to those who take refuge in him" (Proverbs 30:5).

Don't know an ANSWER? Look first in the Bible, then in the back of this book…

The Great Battle

Our fight is not against people on earth.... We are fighting against the spiritual powers of evil in the heavenly world. (EPHESIANS 6:12)

TRIPLE SEARCH:

How many words can you find that are included in ALL THREE of these verses?

Fight the good fight of the faith. Take hold of the eternal life to which you were called when you made your good confession.... (1 TIMOTHY 6:12)

Be strong and let us fight bravely for our people and the cities of our God. The Lord will do what is good in his sight. (1 CHRONICLES 19:13)

I have fought the good fight, I have finished the race, I have kept the faith. (2 TIMOTHY 4:7)

WHO SAID THIS?

Tell who made each of these statements in the Scriptures:

1. "Give me children, or I'll die!" (Genesis 30:1).
2. "Don't be afraid. Am I in the place of God? You intended to harm me, but God intended it for good to accomplish what is now being done, the saving of many lives" (Genesis 50:19).
3. "Out of the eater, something to eat; out of the strong, something sweet" (Judges 14:14).
4. "I cannot carry all these people by myself; the burden is too heavy for me. If this is how you are going to treat me, put me to death right now—if I have found favor in your eyes—and do not let me face my own ruin" (Numbers 11:14-15).
5. "Now I am about to go the way of all the earth. You know with all your heart and soul that not one of all the good promises the Lord your God gave you has failed. Every promise has been fulfilled; not one has failed" (Joshua 23:14).
6. "Get out, get out, you man of blood, you scoundrel! The Lord has repaid you for all the blood you shed in the household of Saul" (2 Samuel 16:7-8).
7. "What they are building—if even a fox climbed up on it, he would break down their wall of stones!" (Nehemiah 4:3).

Store up for yourselves treasures in heaven, where moth and rust do not destroy, and where thieves do not break in and steal.
*(**Jesus,** in MATTHEW 6:20)*

RHYME TIME: Use the rhyme clues to help you tell the missing words to complete Proverbs 2:1-10.

1. My child, believe what I ______. *rhymes with* day
2. And ______ what I command you. Listen to wisdom. *rhymes with* December
3. ______ with all your heart *rhymes with* cry
4. to ______ understanding. *rhymes with* pain
5. Cry ______ for wisdom. *rhymes with* shout
6. ______ for understanding. *rhymes with* leg

7. ______ for it as you would for silver. *rhymes with* church

8. Hunt for it like hidden ______. *rhymes with* pleasure

9. Then you will understand what it means to respect the ______. *rhymes with* sword

10. Then you will begin to ______ God. *rhymes with* grow

11. Only the Lord gives wisdom. Knowledge and understanding ______ from him. *rhymes with* some

12. He ______ up wisdom for those who are honest. *rhymes with* chores

13. Like a ______ he protects those who are innocent. *rhymes with* yield

14. He ______ those who are fair to others. *rhymes with* yards

15. He protects ______ who are loyal to him. *rhymes with* rose

16. Then you will understand what is honest and fair and ______. *rhymes with* sight

17. You will understand what is ______ to do. *rhymes with* wood

18. You will have wisdom in your ______. *rhymes with* art

19. And knowledge will be pleasing to ____. *rhymes with* true

Don't know an ANSWER? Look first in the Bible, then in the back of this book...

ANSWERS

ANSWERS

Faces & Places

1. Joseph 2. Moses 3. Adam and Eve 4. a lions' den in Babylon 5. the Temple in Jerusalem 6. inside the belly of a whale, or large fish 7. Abraham and Sarah

Jesus Our Friend

1. Peter's mother-in-law 2. many tax collectors and "sinners" 3. "The girl is not dead but asleep"; they knew she had died 4. Zacchaeus 5. made an opening in the roof, and lowered the man through it 6. it was too crowded 7. they were silent

Bible Heroes

1. Noah 2. Abraham 3. Jacob 4. Joseph 5. Moses 6. Joshua 7. Rahab 8. Gideon 9. Samson 10. Ruth 11. Hannah 12. Samuel 13. David 14. Jonathan WORK TIME: 1. Adam 2. Noah 3. Joseph 4. Moses 5. Moses 6. Joshua 7. Samuel 8. David 9. Solomon 10. Elijah 11. Daniel 12. Jonah 13. a great fish, or whale

Bible Promises

1. (C) 2. (D) 3. (B) 4. (A)

Bible Miracles

1. "Let there be light" 2. rested 3. one of the man's ribs 4. mud, made from Jesus' saliva and the dirt of the ground 5. a snake 6. a bush 7. his hand 8. Jonah 9. a vine 10. Jesus and Peter 11. Jesus said to it, "May you never bear fruit again"

Knowing God

1. God is light; / in him there is no darkness at all 2. The Lord is my shepherd, / I shall not be in want 3. Great is the Lord, / and most worthy of praise 4. strength 5. rock 6. fortress 7. deliverer 8. rock 9. refuge 10. shield 11. salvation 12. stronghold 13. worthy 14. saved

Born Again

KEY WORD: life FAMOUS QUESTIONS: 1. in jail in Philippi 2. "Repent and be baptized, every one of you, in the name of Jesus Christ for the forgiveness of your sins" 3. like the face of an angel 4. no, He did not answer "Yes" 5. "Do you believe the prophets? I know you do" 6. Saul (later, Paul) 7. from the book of the prophet Isaiah

Be Strong in the Lord

KEY WORD: strong SWORD-SHARPENERS: Be, Arm, The, Therefore, Let, Even

Bible Numbers

1. 99 2. one 3. ten 4. three

5. three 6. three 7. three 8. one (Peter) 9. 153 10. two 11. two 12. three — John, 1 John, 2 John, 3 John, and Revelation 13. two — 1 and 2 Peter 14. at least thirteen — all the letters from Romans through Philemon 15. two — Luke and Acts 16. two 17. five 18. twelve 19. 5,000 men, besides women and children

When Tough Times Come

1. strength 2. trouble 3. fear 4. sea 5. Almighty 6. know 7. God

Children in the Bible

1. heaven 2. stand 3. change 4. humbles GOLD STAR SPECIAL: 1. sky 2. Ten Commandments 3. David 4. Adam and Eve 5. shepherds 6. baptized 7. preached in the desert 8. Jesus rose into heaven 9. Saul 10. Adam named animals

Women in the Bible

1. Mary and Martha 2. Eve 3. Elizabeth 4. Mary Magdalene 4. Naomi 5. Deborah 6. Dorcas 7. Abigail 8. Miriam 9. Rachel 10. Rebekah 11. Sarah

Men in the Bible

1. Zacchaeus 2. Saul 3. Goliath 4. Luke 5. Gideon 6. David 7. Matthew 8. Peter 9. Paul 10. Moses

Our Home in Heaven

1. bride 2. God 3. life 4. name 5. star 6. dressed 7. temple 8. throne

Book, Chapter & Verse

1. John 2. Mark 3. Esther 4. Job 5. Numbers 6. Amos 7. Peter 8. Acts 9. Jude 10. Luke 11. Daniel 12. Titus 13. Romans 14. Judges 15. James 16. Ruth 17. Micah 18. Nahum 19. Haggai 20. Kings 21. Revelation 22. Lamentations or Galatians 23. Habakkuk 24. Proverbs 25. Hebrews 26. Philemon 27. Deuteronomy ROAD TO HAPPINESS: 1. poor 2. kingdom 3. comforted 4. earth 5. thirst 6. mercy 7. heart 8. God 9. theirs

Angels

1. the Garden of Eden 2. Balaam 3. Gabriel 4. shepherds near Bethlehem

Bible Commands

1. You are my friends / if you do what I command you 2. Love your enemies / and pray for those who persecute you 3. Do not judge, or you too will be judged 4. If you love me, /

you will obey what I command 5. Do not worry about tomorrow, / for tomorrow will worry about itself / Each day has enough trouble of its own 6. As the Father has loved me, / so have I loved you / Now remain in my love 7. Let your light shine before men, / that they may see your good deeds / and praise your Father in heaven 8. If someone strikes you on the right cheek, / turn to him the other also 9. If someone forces you to go one mile, / go with him two miles

God Became a Man

1. sinners 2. mercy 3. nations 4. Bethlehem 5. proclaim 6. angels 7. rise 8. born

Jesus Our Leader

1. Father 2. name 3. kingdom 4. heaven 5. today 6. Forgive 7. temptation 8. evil DAY AND NIGHT: 1. Bethany 2. called His disciples to Him and chose twelve to be apostles 3. Nicodemus 4. three 5. Paul

Bold & Brave

1. Nehemiah 2. Esther 3. Job 4. Daniel 5. Daniel 6. Jonah 7. Josiah

All Your Heart

1. Solomon 2. Jesus 3. heart 4. saved

Keep in Mind

KEY WORD: mind

Jesus Our King

1. rock 2. hear Jesus' words but do not put them into practice 3. hear Jesus words and put them into practice EXTRA EXERCISE: 1. Genesis 2. John 3. Psalms 4. Job 5. Joshua 6. Revelation 7. Habakkuk 8. Amos

God's People

1. tree of the knowledge of good and evil 2. red stew; lentil stew 3. Sarah would have a baby son 4. cows 5. lamb 6. yeast, leaven 7. manna 8. quail

The Promised Land

1. Abraham 2. Isaac 3. Jacob WHICH WAY: 1. Sea of Galilee 2. Jordan River 3. Mount of Olives 4. Dead Sea 5. Great Sea

Talking to God

1. Jesus 2. Stephen 3. David 4. Samson 5. Moses 6. Jacob 7. Job 8. Hannah

The Way of Wisdom

Ants, bear, child, dam, Ears, eyes, furnace, Gray, happy, iron, judges, know, lion, medicine, neck, out, prayer, quickly, right, sing, teeth, up, vegetables, wealthy, ox, lazy

The Holy Spirit

1. dove 2. the blowing of a violent wind 3. tongues of fire separating and coming to rest on them 4. in other languages or tongues 5. they declared the wonders of God

The Way of Love

SWORD-SHARPENERS: Look, One, Very, Even

What Happened When

1. 1025 BC 2. AD 30 3. 2091 BC 4. 1526 BC 5. 586 BC

Jesus Our Savior

1. true 2. true 3. true 4. true 5. Father, forgive them, / for they do not know / what they are doing 6. I tell you the truth, / today you will be with me in paradise 7. Dear woman, here is your son 8. Here is your mother 9. My God, my God, / why have you forsaken me? 10. I am thirsty 11. It is finished 12. Father, into your hands / I commit my spirit

Soldiers & Kings

1. Jericho 2. Saul 3. David 4. David 5. Pharaoh's army of the Egyptians 6. Solomon 7. Ahab 8. Josiah 9. Nebuchadnezzar

The Coming Kingdom

1. King, Lord 2. kingdom 3. become 4. Christ 5. ever

Fan the Flame

KEY WORD: see

The Great Battle

KEY WORD: stand 1. Jacob 2. Satan, as a serpent 3. Peter 4. Sarah 5. Samson 6. Herod 7. Saul 8. Ananias and Sapphira 9. they fell down and died

Treasure Chest

1. store 2. treasures 3. moth 4. thieves 5. your 6. heart SWORD-SHARPENERS: Taste, Remember, Every, All, Success, Understand, Reach, Encourage

Faces & Places

1. Eve 2. Cain 3. Abel 4. Seth 5. Adam 6. Absalom 7. Abraham 8. fruit trees 9. fig tree 10. sycamore-fig 11. tamarisk tree

Jesus Our Friend

1. brothers 2. friends 3. We had to celebrate and be glad / because this brother of yours was dead / and is alive again; / he was lost and is found 4. Rejoice with me; / I have found my lost sheep 5. Rejoice with me; / I have found my lost coin 6. A farmer went out to sow his seed 7. A man was going down / from Jerusalem to Jericho, / when he fell into the hands of robbers 8. He would not even look up to heaven, / but beat his breast and said, / "God, have mercy on me, a sinner"

Bible Heroes

1. Zechariah 2. Gabriel 3. Mary 4. Magi (Wise Men) 5. Joseph 6. Joseph 7. John the Baptist 8. the disciples 9. Peter 10. the good Samaritan 11. Zacchaeus 12. Joseph of Arimathea 13. Ananias 14. Paul and Silas 15. John ONE-WORD CLUES: 1. Solomon 2. Elijah 3. Elisha 4. Josiah 5. Shadrach, Meshach, and Abednego 6. Mary 7. Joseph 8. John the Baptist 9. Peter 10. Paul 11. John

Bible Promises

1. (C) 2. (A) 3. (B)

Bible Miracles

1. day 2. night 3. very good 4. So God created man in his own image 5. in the image of God he created him 6. male and female he created them 7. his boat 8. "Put out into deep water, and let down the nets for a catch" 9. "Master, we've worked hard all night and haven't caught anything. But because you say so, I will let down the nets" 10. they caught so many fish their nets began to break 11. "Go away from me, Lord; I am a sinful man"

Knowing God

1. "Do not come any closer. Take off your sandals, for the place where you are standing is holy ground"
2. Abraham, Isaac, and Jacob 3. "I am concerned about their suffering" 4. "I will be with you" 4. "I AM WHO I AM" 5. goodness 6. name 7. presence 8. mercy 9. compassion 10. face

Born Again

1. forgive 2. mouth 3. power 4. Spirit 5. God 6. living 7. becoming 8. everything

Be Strong in the Lord

KEY WORD: grace BLESSINGS FOR EVERYONE: 1. The Lord bless you /

and keep you; / the Lord make his face shine upon you / and be gracious to you; / the Lord turn his face toward you / and give you peace
2. You will be blessed in the city / and blessed in the country… / You will blessed when you come in / and blessed when you go out 3. I will make you into a great nation / and I will bless you; / I will make your name great, / and you will be a blessing / I will bless those who bless you; / and whoever curses you I will curse; / and all peoples on earth / will be blessed through you

Bible Numbers

1. (g) 2. (c) 3. (j) 4. (k) 5. (d) 6. (a) 7. (l) 8. (i) 9. (b) 10. (f) 11. (h) 12. (e) 13. twelve 14. three 15. once

When Tough Times Come

SWORD-SHARPENERS: Heaven, Answer, Rejoice, Death

Children in the Bible

1. Naaman 2. Elisha 3. wash himself seven times in the Jordan River
GOLD STAR SPECIAL: 1. 1 Kings 2. Esther 3. Mark 4. Exodus 5. Malachi 6. Romans 7. Ecclesiastes 8. 1 Peter

Women in the Bible

1. Abigail 2. Esther 3. Hannah 4. Ruth 5. Eve 6. Delilah 7. Martha 8. Rebekah 9. Elizabeth 10. Mary 11. Rhoda

Men in the Bible

1. Peter 2. Peter and Andrew 3. Matthew 4. Peter 5. Peter 6. James 7. Andrew 8. John 9. Peter 10. Thomas 11. John 12. Peter 13. Peter, James, and John 14. Peter 15. Judas

Our Home in Heaven

KEY WORD: you VOICE OF GOD:
1. Satan, the serpent 2. Noah 3. Moses 4. Abraham 5. Adam 6. Moses 7. Abraham

Book, Chapter & Verse

1. good 2. thorny 3. roadside 4. rocky 5. planted it in his field 6. it is the smallest of all seeds 7. grows, and becomes the largest garden plant; becomes a tree that birds can perch in 8. tell it to move, and it will move

Angels

1. Jacob 2. Glory 3. highest 4. earth 5. favor

Bible Commands

1. You shall have no other gods before me 2. You shall not make for yourself an idol 3. You shall not misuse the name of the Lord your God 4. Remember the Sabbath day by keeping it holy 5. Honor your father

and your mother 6. You shall not murder 7. You shall not commit adultery 8. You shall not steal 9. You shall not give false testimony against your neighbor 10. You shall not covet

God Became a Man

1. forgiven 2. house 3. praise 4. trying 5. understand 6. believe 7. Sabbath 8. son 9. you 10. kings 11. hour 12. drink 13. capture 14. slow

Jesus Our Leader

1. He went to him / and bandaged his wounds, / pouring on oil and wine / Then he put the man on his own donkey, / took him to an inn / and took care of him 2. Well done, good and faithful servant! / You have been faithful / with a few things; / I will put you in charge / of many things / Come and share your master's happiness 3. I tell you that to everyone who has, / more will be given / but as for the one who has nothing / even what he has / will be taken away 4. My oxen and fattened cattle / have been butchered / and everything is ready / Come to the wedding banquet 5. Shouldn't you have had mercy / on your fellow servant / just as I had on you?

Bold & Brave

KEY WORD: light BRAVE WORDS: 1. Esther 2. Joshua 3. Caleb 4. Peter and John 5. Rahab 6. Jonathan 7. Nehemiah

All Your Heart

TRIPLE SEARCH: heart, face

Keep in Mind

KEY WORD: truth

Jesus Our King

1. This gospel of the kingdom / will be preached in the whole world / as a testimony to all nations / and then the end will come 2. The righteous will shine like the sun / in the kingdom of their Father EXTRA EXERCISE: 1. Revelation 2. Isaiah 3. 2 Samuel 4. Daniel 5. Jeremiah and 2 Kings

God's People

1. Zechariah 2. Xerxes 3. Adam 4. Joseph 5. Jacob 6. Isaac 7. Boaz 8. Abraham 9. Eve 10. Sarah 11. Rachel 12. Elizabeth 13. Hannah 14. Mary 15. Jacob 16. Adam 17. Jesse 18. Abraham 19. Isaac 20. Zebedee 21. Zechariah 22. Saul 23. Noah

The Promised Land

1. Moses 2. honey 3. chosen WHICH WAY: 1. Nazareth 2. Babylon 3. Sodom and Gomorrah 4. Negev Desert 5. Egypt 6. Rome

Talking to God

1. Jesus 2. Ezra 3. Elisha 4. Elisha

5. Elijah 6. Elijah 7. David
8. Abraham's servant, Eliezer

The Way of Wisdom

afraid, brother, calm, destroys, easy, foolish, gift, hide, innocent, joy, kill, learn, Money, nation, others, praised, questions, rich, sad, thinks, unfriendly, vanishes, word, extremely, young, gaze

The Holy Spirit

KEY WORD: one

The Way of Love

SWORD-SHARPENERS: Heal, Each, All, Rescue, Take

What Happened When

1. 2065 BC 2. AD 44 3. 1446 BC
4. 1010 BC 5. 848 BC

Jesus Our Savior

1. The Son of Man came / to seek and to save what was lost 2. I tell you the truth, / if anyone keeps my word, / he will never see death
3. This is the blood of my covenant / which is poured out for many / for the forgiveness of sins 4. I am the resurrection and the life / He who believes in me will live / even though he dies; / and whoever believes in me / will never die 5. The man who loves his life will lose it / while the man who hates his life / in this world / will keep it for eternal life 6. The work of God is this: / to believe in the one he has sent 7. I am the bread of life / He who comes to me will never go hungry, / and he who believes in me / will never be thirsty

Soldiers & Kings

1. David 2. Solomon 3. Pharaoh
4. Joshua 5. Jeroboam 6. Naaman
7. Saul 8. David 9. David

The Coming Kingdom

1. The sun will be darkened, / and the moon will not give its light; / the stars will fall from the sky / and the heavenly bodies will be shaken
2. Therefore keep watch, / because you do not know on what day / your Lord will come

Fan the Flame

SWORD-SHARPENERS: Fight, Lead, Aim, Make, Everyone

The Great Battle

1. Satan 2. He will be thrown into a lake of burning sulfur to suffer torment forever WHO SAID THIS:
1. Pharaoh 2. John the Baptist
3. God 4. Peter 5. Zacchaeus 6. people of Israel 7. Aaron 8. David

Treasure Chest

SWORD-SHARPENERS: Give, Open, Let, Delight KINGDOM TREASURE:
1. sold everything he had 2. sold everything he had

Faces & Places

1. Bethlehem 2. Jerusalem 3. Jesus 4. Goshen 5. Shiloh 6. Zion 7. Judah 8. Israel

Jesus Our Friend

SWORD-SHARPENERS: Just, Even, See, Until, Salt JESUS AND THE HOLY SPIRIT: 1. When the Spirit of truth comes, / he will guide you into all truth 2. The Spirit will take from what is mine / and make it known to you 3. I will ask the Father / and he will give you another Counselor / to be with you forever / the Spirit of truth 4. The Counselor, the Holy Spirit / whom the Father will send in my name / will teach you all things / and remind you of everything / I have said to you 5. If you then, though you are evil / know how to give good gifts to your children / how much more will your Father in heaven / give the Holy Spirit / to those who ask him!

Bible Heroes

1. Elijah 2. Samson 3. Elijah 4. Paul 5. Moses 6. Shadrach, Meshach, and Abednego 7. Peter 8. Gideon 9. Jeremiah 10. David 11. Noah 12. Zechariah SHOUTS IN THE BIBLE: 1. Jesus 2. Goliath 3. Paul 4. King Nebuchadnezzar 5. the prophets of Baal 6. the rulers of the Philistines 7. Esau 8. the people of Jerusalem 9. the people of Jerusalem 10. Jesus

Bible Promises

1. (A) 2. (B) 3. (C)

Bible Miracles

1. sun 2. light 3. stars 4. oceans 5. sky 6. ants 7. roses 8. sharks 9 seven 10. a few 11. 4,000, besides women and children

Knowing God

1. my Father 2. Father 3. God 4. faith 5. Holy 6. spirit 7. grace 8. faithful 9. righteous

Born Again

TRIPLE SEARCH: pure, heart WHAT'S THAT I HEAR: 1. the bones coming to life 2. the Holy Spirit 3. "Abraham! Abraham! Do not lay a hand on the boy"

Be Strong in the Lord

1. Jesus 2. David 3. Paul GOLD STAR SPECIAL: 1. John 2. 1 Peter 3. Acts 4. Matthew 5. Galatians 6. 1 John

Bible Numbers

1. two hundred million
2. Methuselah 3. 969 years 4. Jared
5. 962 years 6. Noah 7. 950 years

When Tough Times Come

KEY WORD: discipline

Children in the Bible

1. Moses 2. Peter 3. Abel 4. Esau
5. James 6. Rachel 7. Mary
8. Merab 9. Simeon and Levi
10. Lazarus 11. Laban
12. Absalom

Women in the Bible

1. Michal 2. Delilah 3. Michal
4. Hagar 5. Mary 6. Hannah
7. Naomi 8. Deborah 9. Rahab
10. Miriam

Men in the Bible

1. Moses and Elijah 2. Blessed is the man who fears the Lord 3. Blessed is the man who finds wisdom
4. Blessed is the man who makes the Lord his trust 5. Abraham
6. Samson 7. David 8. Daniel
9. Samuel 10. Peter 11. Noah
12. Moses

Our Home in Heaven

1. guiding 2. treasures VOICE OF GOD: 1. Eve 2. Elijah 3. Paul
4. Samuel 5. Moses 6. Miriam and Aaron

Book, Chapter & Verse

1. Genesis 2. Exodus 3. Exodus
4. Judges 5. John 6. Acts
7. Revelation 8. John 9. Revelation
10. 2 Timothy 11. Daniel 12. 1 Corinthians 13. Genesis
14. Proverbs 15. Acts 16. Colossians
17. Exodus

Angels

1. Philip 2. Cornelius 3. Peter
4. Paul 5. the apostles

Bible Commands

1. a calf 2. from their earrings
3. "These are your gods, O Israel, who brought you up out of Egypt"
4. prayed for them 5. he threw them down and broke them 3. burned it in the fire, ground it to powder, scattered the powder in water, and made the Israelites drink it

God Became a Man

1. Jesus 2. Jesus 3. someone else
4. Jesus 5. someone else 6. Son of Man 7. night 8. son 9. man
10. heaven 11. glory 12. nations
13. dominion 14. destroyed

Jesus Our Leader

1. turned water into wine 2. Peter said Jesus is the Christ 3. washed their feet 4. If anyone would come after me / he must deny himself / and take up his cross daily / and follow me 5. I am the light of the world / Whoever follows me / will never walk in darkness / but will have the light of life 6. Whoever serves me must follow me / and where I am / my servant also will be 7. I have come into the world as a light / so that no one who believes in me / should stay in darkness 8. Heaven and earth will pass away / but my words will never pass away

Bold & Brave

1. strong 2. separate WHO SAID THIS: 1. God 2. Jacob 3. Jesus 4. Elisha 5. Gabriel 6. Isaac 7. Jesus

All Your Heart

KEY WORD: heart

Keep in Mind

SWORD-SHARPENERS: Make, If, No, Discipline

Jesus Our King

1. Peter 2. Pilate 3. Peter 4. the church in Ephesus 5. the church in Smyrna 6. the church in Pergamum 7. the church in Thyatira 8. the church in Sardis 9. the church in Philadelphia 10. the church in Laodicea

God's People

1. Abraham (God) 2. Sarai (God) 3. Israel (God) 4. Peter (Jesus) 5. Paul 6. Abraham 7. Isaac 8. Esau 9. Jacob 10. Reuben, Simeon, Levi, Judah, Dan, Naphtali, Gad, Asher, Issachar, Zebulun, Joseph, Benjamin

The Promised Land

1. Nebo 2. he would die there 3. life 4. long 5. land WHICH WAY: 1. Mount Carmel 2. Damascus 3. Jericho 4. Bethany 5. Moab 6. Red Sea 7. Philistia

Talking to God

SWORD-SHARPENERS: Praise, Remember, All, You EXTRA EXERCISE: 1. 2 Samuel 2. Ruth 3. Matthew 4. Judges 5. Lamentations 6. Jonah 7. 2 John

The Way of Wisdom

animals, beating, crown, dishonesty, evil, forget, gentle, hate, ignores, jealousy, king, lead, mother, nothing, oil,

poor, quiet, respect, sister, treasure, unpunished, value, wealth, six, you, amazing

The Holy Spirit

1. love 2. joy 3. peace 4. patience 5. kindness 6. goodness 7. faithfulness 8. gentleness 9. self-control

The Way of Love

1. patient 2. kind 3. envy 4. boast 5. proud 6. rude 7. self-seeking 8. angered 9. wrongs 10. evil 11. truth 12. protects 13. trusts 14. hopes 15. perseveres 16. fails

What Happened When

1. 1105 BC 2. 2006 BC 3. 740 BC 4. AD 57 5. 1446 BC

Jesus Our Savior

1. the devil, Satan 2. free SWORD-SHARPENERS: Seek, After, Very, It, One, Rise

Soldiers & Kings

1. Ehud 2. Shamgar 3. Deborah 4. Gideon 5. Abimelech 6. Jephthah

The Coming Kingdom

KEY WORD: new

Fan the Flame

1. the Spirit 2. apostles 3. prophets 4. evangelists 5. pastors and teachers

The Great Battle

1. Satan, and anyone whose name was not found written in the book of life 2. Jesus 3. forever 4. fire WHO SAID THIS: 1. a man born blind 2. the Magi (Wise Men) 3. Jesus 4. Mary 5. the people of Israel 6. Satan, the serpent 7. Jesus 8. Pontius Pilate 9. Pharaoh

Treasure Chest

1. precious 2. above 3. advice 4. wealth 5. way 6. poor 7. time 8. made

Faces & Places

1. Sarah 2. Cain 3. Esau 4. Ishmael 5. John 6. Amnon 7. Hannah 8. Anna 9. Asa 10. Nabal and Laban

Jesus Our Friend

KEY WORD: love NAMES OF JESUS: 1. Bread of Life 2. Light of the World 3. Good Shepherd 4. Resurrection and the Life 5. the Way and the Truth and the Life 6. Vine

Bible Heroes

1. Jesus 2. Jesus 3. Elijah 4. Elisha 5. Jesus 6. Rahab's 7. Achan 8. the smoke of their burning city 9. the Book of the Law 10. it stayed still for about a full day 11. block the mouth of the cave with rocks VOICE OF GOD: 1. Cain 2. Ananias 3. Elijah 4. Jacob 5. Jacob 6. Samuel

Bible Promises

1. (C) 2. (B) 3. (A)

Bible Miracles

1. "the king of Egypt will not let you go unless a mighty hand compels him" 2. No 3. He went to a mountain by Himself 4. so that others would believe that God had appeared to Moses 5. light 6. sky 7. dry ground, oceans, plants, trees 8. sun, moon, stars 9. fish, birds 10. land animals, man

Knowing God

1. Moses 2. gentle whisper 3. the Samaritan woman at Jacob's well 4. the Sadducees 5. His disciples 6. the Pharisees 7. a rich ruler 8. Nicodemus 9. the Jews in Jerusalem

Born Again

KEY WORD: praise WHO SAID THIS: 1. Joseph 2. Pilate 3. Paul 4. Judas 5. Abigail 6. Jesus' disciples

Be Strong in the Lord

1. I am not ashamed of the gospel / because it is the power of God / for the salvation of everyone who believes 2. Consider it pure joy, my brothers / whenever you face trials of many kinds FAMOUS QUESTIONS: 1. David 2. Pilate 3. God 4. Moses 5. Peter 6. Jesus 7. Judas 8. the Samaritan woman at Jacob's well 9. Nicodemus 10. Peter

Bible Numbers

1. three 2. 300 cubits 3. 30 cubits 4. 50 cubits 5. 600 years old 6. seven 7. two 8. forty 9. eight 10. 150 days 11. forty days 12. seven days 13. seven days

14. just over twelve months 15. 350 years 16. 950 years

When Tough Times Come

KEY WORD: suffer

Children in the Bible

1. Joab 2. David 3. Jesus 4. Abraham 5. Miriam 6. a girl from Israel who was a servant of Naaman's wife 7. Isaac 8. some youths calling out to Elisha 9. Samuel 10. Samuel 11. the son of the Shunammite woman 12. Paul's nephew

Women in the Bible

1. Naomi 2. Rachel 3. Adam 4. because she would be "the mother of all living" GOLD STAR SPECIAL: 1. 1 Samuel 2. Malachi 3. Nahum 4. Esther 5. Jonah

Men in the Bible

1. Peter 2. Peter, James, and John 3. Andrew 4. James 5. James and John 6. John 7. Thomas 8. Peter 9. Philip 10. Nathanael 11. Matthew 12. Peter

Our Home in Heaven

1. Enoch 2. Elijah 3. Jesus was taken up, and a cloud hid Him from their sight WHO SAID THIS: 1. Jonah 2. Martha 3. God 4. the Jews in Jerusalem 5. an angel at Jesus' tomb 6. Jesus 7. Peter 8. Moses 9. Jesus

Book, Chapter & Verse

1. 1 Kings 2. Luke 3. John 4. Judges 5. Ezekiel 6. Daniel 7. Hebrews 8. Luke 9. Job 10. Joshua 11. Ruth 12. Matthew 13. 1 John 14. Isaiah 15. Ephesians 16. Romans 17. Ezekiel 18. Song of Solomon 19. Nehemiah 20. Genesis 21. James

Angels

1. Joseph 2. Elijah 3. Abraham 4. John 5. Mary 6. Zechariah

Bible Commands

1. Love 2. God 3. all 4. your 5. commandment 6. neighbor 7. Give to the one who asks you to / and do not turn away / the one who wants to borrow from you 8. Seek first his kingdom and his righteousness / and all these things / will be given to you as well 9. When you give to the needy / do not let your left hand know / what your right is doing 10. The harvest is plentiful / but the workers are few / Ask the Lord of the harvest, therefore / to send out workers into his harvest field

God Became a Man

1. someone else 2. Jesus 3. someone else 4. someone else 5. Jesus 6. Jesus 7. someone else 8. Jesus 9. Jesus 10. someone else 11. Jesus 12. Jesus 13. someone else 14. someone else 15. Jesus

Jesus Our Leader

1. My food is to do / the will of him who sent me / and to finish his work 2. Whoever does the will / of my Father in heaven / is my brother and sister and mother 3. Shepherd 4. he goes to find it 5. puts it on his shoulders and goes home 6. calls his friends and neighbors to celebrate together

Bold & Brave

TRIPLE SEARCH: not, be, afraid
EXTRA EXERCISE: 1. 1 John 2. Daniel 3. 2 Chronicles 4. Hebrews 5. 2 Kings 6. Ezra

All Your Heart

KEY WORD: hope

Keep in Mind

SWORD-SHARPENERS: Put, Each, All, Come, Eyes

Jesus Our King

1. His disciples 2. His disciples 3. His disciples 4. the buyers and sellers in the Temple 5. Zacchaeus 6. His disciples 7. a Canaanite woman 8. His disciples 9. Peter 10. James and John 11. a fig tree 12. His disciples 13. Paul 14. the Pharisees

God's People

1. Jacob 2. Job 3. Saul 4. Laban 5. Bethuel 6. David 7. Jochebed 8. Leah 9. Joseph 10. Lappidoth 11. Hosea 12. Elkanah 13. Herod 14. Ahab 15. Jacob 16. David 17. Elimelech 18. Aquila 19. Moses 20. Nabal 21. David 22. Uriah 23. David

The Promised Land

1. The Lord himself goes before you 2. and will be with you 3. he will never leave you 4. nor forsake you 5. Do not be afraid 6. do not be discouraged WHICH WAY: 1. Ephesus 2. Samaria 3. Assyria 4. Mount Nebo 5. Edom 6. Mount Sinai 7. Emmaus

Talking to God

1. the eleven apostles 2. Jeremiah 3. David 4. the believers in Jerusalem 5. Hezekiah 6. Jonah 7. Jesus 8. Manoah 9. Samson

The Way of Wisdom

advice, bold, corrected, disciplines,

enemy, friend, generous, Humility, integrity, justice, kind, listening, mouth, neighbor, obey, Patience, quarrels, rewarded, secret, Trust, understand, voice, work, exalts, years, zealous

The Holy Spirit

1. love 2. joy 3. peace 4. patience 5. kindness 6. goodness 7. faithfulness 8. gentleness 9. self-control

The Way of Love

SWORD-SHARPENERS: Great, One, Day

What Happened When

1. AD 57 2. 997 BC 3. 1898 BC 4. 1443 BC 5. 622 BC

Jesus Our Savior

1. Whoever believes in me / as the Scripture has said / streams of living water / will flow from within him 2. It is not the healthy who need a doctor / but the sick REPUTATION: 1. James and John 2. David 3. Herod 4. Judah 5. Satan 6. Barnabas 7. Abraham 8. Ishmael 9. David 10. Abraham 11. Abraham 12. Gideon 13. Elijah 14. Abraham 15. Zebulun 16. Naphtali 17. Dan 18. Benjamin 19. Jesus

Soldiers & Kings

1. King Nebuchadnezzar of Babylon 2. Pharaoh of Egypt 3. the Lord's FAMOUS ANSWERS: 1. Adam 2. Cain 3. Peter 4. Jesus 5. the man born blind, and healed by Jesus 6. David 7. Jonathan 8. Peter 9. John the Baptist

The Coming Kingdom

1. collected them in baskets 2. threw them away 3. they will be thrown into the fiery furnace, "where there will be weeping and gnashing of teeth"

Fan the Flame

SWORD-SHARPENERS: He, Once, Let, Year

The Great Battle

1. salvation 2. the Spirit 3. faith 4. righteousness 5. truth 6. gospel of peace

Treasure Chest

KEY WORD: noble WHO SAID THIS: 1. Elijah 2. the people of Egypt 3. Jesus 4. Jesus 5. Samuel 6. Paul

Faces & Places

1. Samuel 2. Moses 3. Solomon 4. Hezekiah 5. Elizabeth 6. Nebuchadnezzar 7. Jezebel 8. Zechariah 9. Hezekiah 10. Zechariah (prophet), Ezra (priest), Ezekiel (priest and prophet) 11. Eleazar

Jesus Our Friend

1. Where two or three come together in my name / there am I with them 2. Whatever you did for one / of the least of these brothers of mine / you did for me 3. Peace I leave with you / my peace I give you / I do not give to you as the world gives / Do not let your hearts be troubled / and do not be afraid 4. Here I am!. I stand at the door and knock / If anyone hears my voice / and opens the door / I will come in and eat with him / and he with me 5. God is Spirit / and his worshipers must worship / in spirit and in truth 6. When a man believes in me / he does not believe in me only / but in the one who sent me 7. What God has joined together / let man not separate

Bible Heroes

1. anointed king 2. arrested 3. put in jail 4. Apollos 5. his staff 6. sling and stone 7. stars 8. trumpet 9. bread 10. weapons 11. tambourine 12. Goliath's head

FAMOUS QUESTIONS: 1. God 2. Jesus' disciples 3. Abraham 4. the chief priests and elders 5. Jesus 6. Peter 7. Zechariah 8. Elkanah 9. Samuel

Bible Promises

1. (B) 2. (C) 3. (A)

Bible Miracles

1. blood 2. frogs 3. gnats 4. flies 5. livestock 6. boils 7. hail 8. locusts 9. darkness 10. death to the firstborn of all people and cattle

Knowing God

1. Abraham 2. Theophilus 3. God's 4. John 5. Genesis 6. Isaiah 7. Deuteronomy 8. Hebrews 9. Psalms 10. 1 Samuel

Born Again

KEY WORD: joy DREAMS IN THE BIBLE: 1. Joseph 2. Pharaoh 3. a Midianite soldier at the time of Gideon 4. Paul 5. Jacob 6. Nebuchadnezzar 7. Solomon 8. Joseph of Nazareth

Be Strong in the Lord

1. Jesus 2. Moses VOICE OF GOD: 1. David 2. Samuel 3. Ahab 4. Elijah 5. Paul

Bible Numbers

1. Genesis, Exodus, Leviticus, Numbers, Deuteronomy, 1

Chronicles, 2 Chronicles, Psalms, Proverbs, Ecclesiastes, Lamentations, Revelation 2. 1 & 2 Samuel, 1 & 2 Kings, 1 & 2 Chronicles, 1 & 2 Corinthians, 1 & 2 Thessalonians, 1 & 2 Timothy, 1 & 2 Peter, 1, 2, & 3 John, and...Numbers! 3. Job 4. 1 and 2 Thessalonians, and Lamentations 5. Ruth, Ezra, Joel, Amos, Mark, Luke, John, Acts, 1 John, 2 John, 3 John, Jude

When Tough Times Come

SWORD-SHARPENERS: Be, Remain, Answer, Very, Everything

Children in the Bible

1. Solomon 2. John the Baptist GOLD STAR SPECIAL: 1. 1 Thessalonians 2. Hosea 3. James 4. Ecclesiastes 5. Proverbs 6. Psalms 7. Colossians 8. Ephesians

Women in the Bible

1. sons 2. Sarah 3. Tamar, Rahab, Ruth, Bathsheba (wife of Uriah) 4. Priscilla 5. Bathsheba 6. Job 7. Pilate 8. Potiphar 9. Naaman 10. Manoah 11. Lot 12. Jeroboam

Men in the Bible

1. Peter 2. Nathanael 3. Peter 4. John 5. Peter 6. John 7. Peter 8. James 9. Bartholomew, Nathanael 10. Matthew, Levi 11. Simon 12. Judas, Thaddaeus 13. Peter 14. James and John 15. Peter 16. Nathanael 17. Philip 18. Andrew 19. Thomas 20. Peter 21. Judas 22. Andrew 23. Peter and John 24. Peter 25. Peter 26. Peter 27. Peter and John 28. John 29. Peter and John 30. James and John 31. Nathanael 32. Andrew and Philip 33. Thomas 34. Judas Iscariot 35. James and John 36. Matthias

Our Home in Heaven

1. And he will send his angels / with a loud trumpet call / and they will gather his elect / from the four winds / from one end of the heavens / to the other 2. You also must be ready / because the Son of Man will come / at an hour when you do not expect him WHO SAID THIS: 1. Rebekah 2. Jesus 3. Martha 4. Simeon 5. Jacob

Book, Chapter & Verse

1. Psalm 119, with 176 verses 2. Psalm 117, with two verses 3. John 3:16 4. Psalms, with 150 chapters

Angels

1. Jacob 2. Hagar 3. Daniel 4. John

Bible Commands

KEY WORD: love BIG TEN: 1. gods before me 2. an idol 3. the name of the Lord your God 4. the Sabbath day 5. your father and your mother 6. murder 7. commit adultery 8. steal 9. give false testimony against your neighbor 10. covet

God Became a Man

1. think 2. Christ 3. God 4. gave 5. nothing 6. man 7. humbled 8. death 9. raised 10. name 11. knee 12. everyone 13. Lord 14. bring 15. Father

Jesus Our Leader

1. Now that I, your Lord and Teacher / have washed your feet / you also should wash one another's feet 2. I have set you an example / that you should do as I have done for you 3. Now that you know these things / you will be blessed if you do them EXTRA EXERCISE: 1. Judges 2. Exodus 3. Genesis 4. Song of Solomon 5. Habakkuk 6. Deuteronomy 7. Luke

Bold & Brave

1. Jael 2. Samson 3. Benaiah 4. Abishai WHO SAID THIS: 1. Jacob 2. Jesus 3. the Queen of Sheba 4. Pilate 5. Jesus 6. Father Abraham 7. Esau 8. God

All Your Heart

KEY WORD: peace

Keep in Mind

SWORD-SHARPENERS: Teach, Hear, If, Never, Knowing

Jesus Our King

1. Judas Iscariot 2. a leper 3. His disciples 4. Thomas 5. Peter 6. I am the Alpha and the Omega / the First and the Last / the Beginning and the End 7. I am the Root / and the Offspring of David / the bright Morning Star 8. I am the Alpha and the Omega / who was, and who is / and who is to come / the Almighty 9. I am the Living One / I was dead / and behold I am alive for ever and ever!. and I hold the keys / of death and Hades

God's People

1. Jochebed 2. Rahab 3. Hagar 4. Rachel 5. Naomi 6. Leah 7. Eunice 8. Gideon 9. Terah 10. Buzi 11. Eli 12. Amoz 13. Hilkiah 14. Obed 15. Nun 16. Haran 17. Jonathan 18. Lot 19. Joseph 20. Amram 21. Lamech 22. Boaz 23. Solomon 24. Manoah 25. Elkanah 26. Kish 27. David

The Promised Land

1. ten of the twelve spies which Moses sent into Canaan 2. God WHICH WAY: 1. Shiloh 2. Gilgal 3. Heshbon 4. Tekoa 5. Hebron 6. Ziklag 7. Ashdod 8. Joppa

Talking to God

1. Joshua 2. a Pharisee 3. a tax collector 4. Daniel 5. Nehemiah 6. Solomon 7. Jabez 8. Hezekiah

The Way of Wisdom

add, broken, call, deliver, everywhere, far, God, house, instruction, join, kiss, loves, motives, nest, outdoor, path, quarrelsome, rare, succeed, trouble, upright, victory, weighs, mixed, yields, zeal

The Holy Spirit

1. Peter 2. Peter 3. Peter

The Way of Love

1. Boaz 2. John the Baptist 3. David

What Happened When

1. 1406 BC 2. 553 BC 3. AD 35 4. 1805 BC 5. 959 BC

Jesus Our Savior

KEY WORD: faith MASTER'S WORDS: 1. His disciples 2. a woman sick with bleeding 3. Martha 4. Jerusalem 5. Peter 6. Peter, James, and John 7. Mary, His mother 8. John 9. Thomas

Soldiers & Kings

1. Temple guards in Jerusalem 2. the Roman governor's soldiers in Jerusalem 3. a centurion in Jerusalem 4. the commander of the Roman soldiers' barracks in Jerusalem 5. Pharaoh 6. David 7. Samson 8. Goliath 9. Joab 10. Joab 11. a centurion in Capernaum

The Coming Kingdom

1. Nation will rise against nation / and kingdom against kingdom 2. He who stands firm to the end / will be saved 3. They will see the Son of Man / coming on the clouds of the sky / with power and great glory

Fan the Flame

SWORD-SHARPENERS: Father, Is, Rise, Every

The Great Battle

TRIPLE SEARCH: the, good, fight
WHO SAID THIS: 1. Rachel 2. Joseph 3. Samson 4. Moses 5. Joshua 6. Shimei 7. Tobiah

Treasure Chest

1. say 2. remember 3. Try 4. gain 5. out 6. Beg 7. Search 8. treasure 9. Lord 10. know 11. come 12. stores 13. shield 14. guards 15. those 16. right 17. good 18. heart 19. you

If you accept my words
and store up my commands within you,
turning your ear to wisdom
and applying your heart to understanding,
and if you call out for insight
and cry aloud for understanding,
and if you look for it as for silver
and search for it as for hidden treasure,
then you will understand the fear of the Lord
and find the knowledge of God.

PROVERBS 2:1-5

"More desirable than gold... and sweeter than honey..."

That's what Psalm 19 says about Bible truths—
the same rich truths presented just for kids
in Questar's **Gold'n'Honey Books**

OTHER TITLES:

The Beginner's Bible
Timeless Children's Stories

The Early Reader's Bible
"I Can Read" Bible Stories

What Would Jesus Do?
IN HIS STEPS Retold for Children

The Beginner's Devotional

My First Step Bible

The Bible Tells Me So
The Beginner's Guide to Loving & Understanding God's Word

My ABC Bible Memory Book

My Best Bible Word Book Ever

The Bible Animal Storybook